Written by Alana Marie

Copyright 2014 © Alana Marie All Rights Reserved

ISBN-10: 1503000680

Pick a Struggle Cupcake Blog

Where it all started.

www.PickaStruggleCupcake.com

TABLE OF CONTENTS

Introduction   4

With Love and Gratitude   5

The Journal   9

The Gloves   12

Twilight   16

Shooting Stars   21

The Silver Screen   26

Fireworks   29

The Piano   32

Smile   36

Free   39

The Warrior   42

Going In Means Coming Out   43

The Bird   46

The Last Word   49

Regret   53

The Carnival   56

What do I Value?   63

To See It Coming   66

The Mighty Oak   71

Under the Stars   74

The Red Balloons   78

The Flying Duck Bar   80

The Swing   87

Postcards   92

To Be Normal   97

Organized Chaos   100

Better Not Bitter   104

The Zoo   108

Appreciate the Little Things   113

The Hourglass   116

The Edge   120

A Misplaced Memory   121

Gone Too Soon   126

Just Listen   130

Camping   133

Etheltrude Isabella   136

The Pistachio Green Bicycle   145

Letting Go   148

The Good Stuff   151

Big Top Blues   155

Albert O'Malley   157

The Fountain   165

The Attic   170

Cupcakes & Snowflakes   **174**

About the Author   **178**

Introduction

For all of my days, I have dreamed of becoming an author; of writing remarkable stories about love, passion and adventure. I imagined frigid, winter evenings nestled in my favorite leather chair, snuggled inside of my mother's frayed but cozy, flannel blanket. Watching the snowflakes dance outside my window, with the moon shining just bright enough to make them sparkle and shine, I would write my stories and be at peace.

With the publication of this book, my dream has become a reality. My heart beats wildly at the thought of each book venturing out into the unknown to find its way into your hands, someone who will give it life as the first page is turned. I can only hope you will delight in reading the stories of my life, loves, and struggles as much as I have adored composing each of them.

Alana Marie

With Love and Gratitude

I must take a moment to thank a few people. I begin with my mother, Helen, who held my hand through my darkest days and taught me how to beat my demons, one battle at a time. Thank you, Diana, my sister and my best friend, for always standing behind me at the ready, with a gentle push or a kick in the behind. To Charity Wright, my creative writing instructor; thank you for giving me the courage and resolution to pursue my passion for writing outside of the classroom. Without the confidence you instilled in me, this book would not exist. I must thank my dear friend, Amanda Gammons, for convincing me to take a chance and chase this dream while pointing me in the direction of the starting line. Lastly, I must smile and thank my Snowflake for creating a passion in my heart which will both inspire and propel me to astounding heights. You are, indeed, my soul mate.

In addition I would like to thank Shari Yantes my personal development coach for her endless support, Carla Wynn Hall for putting together this publication, Tiffany Tillman for editing the manuscript and a very special thank you to Heidi Kempisty who designed our book cover.

Thank you all for the love and support you have shown me for it has undeniably fueled this fantasy. I am both grateful and humbled.

"Alana's writing is a breath of fresh air. Her stories strike a chord with people of all different backgrounds, histories and genders. There's a little something for everyone in each story she produces. Above all, the pure fact that this woman has found her dream again and is following it through is inspiration for even the uninspirable. "Pick a Struggle, Cupcake" should be a staple on any bookshelf. Thank you Alana for the exceptional stories about growth, loss and motivation"

~Ashley Suzanne~

Author of the Amazon Bestselling Destined Series and Amazon Editor's Pick for Debut Novel, Mirage

"Alana Faulk not only knows what it's like to live through pain, but also to overcome it like an eagle on her first majestic flight. I am astounded at her descriptive and tangible stories and how she makes them come alive. I believe Faulk to be a brilliant writer. Her book, Pick a Struggle Cupcake, will challenge and inspire you to have the courage and strength to come ALIVE with a life that's more meaningful and more beautiful than the one you're currently in."

~Kellie Frazier

*Founder of Connecting LLC Website: **www.KellieFrazier.com***

"Alana Marie is a very gifted writer who uses her talent to draw you in, you'll feel like you're part of the story. When you read her stories, you'll believe she is talking to you, about you or about your life. Alana shares freely the feelings and emotions that we experience in everyday life in a very poetic way. Her writing will make you reflect, experience emotions and think deeply. Alana Maria is an inspiration, an author to follow, her writing is not just something to keep in your library; it's something to experience every day. Alana will help you realize the extraordinary experiences in your ordinary life."

~**Shari Yantes**

Motivational Speaker, Author, Personal Success Coach & Trainer Website: ***www.shariyantes.com***

"I have tears in my eyes, what a GREAT testament to perseverance!!! Thanks for sharing! That smile shines even brighter now!" ~ **Kim G.**

"You are such a powerful and inspiring woman. I am so proud to have read your story. You inspire myself and so many more out there. I'm not having a good day at all today, the weather and such but then I read your story and immediately had a huge smile on my face. You go girl! You freakin' rock!" ~ **Lindsay S.**

Oh my gosh!!! You have done Wonderful!!! And just reading your stories gives me so much Love for you as a Fighter and a Terrific Person in Life. You speaking about nesting in a cozy chair on a Beautiful Winter Eve just took me there!!! Thank you for sharing ~ **Angela S.**

"Your writing is captivating! Love to read your words. I will definitely buy the book. It will make nice Christmas gifts." ~**Helen W.**

"Such a remarkable journey you have traveled. Congratulations to you - I know it hasn't been easy and you had to have had some bumps in the road at times; however, you have overcome all of this. God bless you in your new life." ~**Mildred L.**

"You made me cry reading this story...Please keep going with both your journey in life, your writing and being such a wonderful woman who shares her heart with us. Thank you again" ~ **Carole R.**

"You're an amazing woman. I am so glad I fell upon your website today. I am proud and out and I am on my weight loss journey. I am so thankful for people like you who can write so we can all relate. Just wanted to say thank you!" ~**Kristen**

Cuddle Up and Enjoy

The Journal

"When I tipped the scales at three hundred pounds, I lost the vision, and somewhere between three hundred fifty and four hundred, I lost the passion. When I finally peaked at five hundred twenty eight pounds, well, I lost all hope."

Rummaging through a multitude of boxes in the back of my garage today, I searched eagerly for something I hadn't seen in quite a while. Suddenly, I spotted it there at the bottom of a carton and grinned. Reaching down, I wrapped my fingers around it—the little brown journal which had hoarded all of my thoughts and ideas so many years ago. The leather cover still felt as smooth and soft as butter as I pulled it out and hugged it close to my heart. Feeling as though I had rediscovered a long lost friend, I smiled as I recalled the afternoon which had warranted my splurging on such an auspicious gift for myself. Young and fearless, I was convinced I had the world by the tail.

Heading off to Central Michigan University in the springtime of my youth, I was about to do something with my life; something significant …something extraordinary. My dream was simple: simply write and have my stories published.

Determined to rise each day and settle myself into a big wicker chair on a balcony facing Lake Michigan, I would impetuously pen great volumes of stories and tales from early morning's dawn until twilight kissed the horizon. Excitedly, I would create pages upon pages of wonderful words that would one day fill leather bound books crammed upon shelves of libraries and bookstores for miles around. People would scramble to purchase each and every new release. They would lock themselves away in their bedrooms, reading and relishing every chapter until late into the evening when they fell asleep with my book resting open upon their chest.

My simple words of wit and wisdom would reach so many people and change so many lives. Yes, I had a calling and I realized it.

Sadly, things don't always go as planned. Real life gets in the way. The addictions to food and drink wrapped their powerful arms around me and held me captive for the next twenty years. I ate and drank myself silly as the pounds piled up and the dreams slipped away. When I tipped the scales at three hundred pounds, I lost the vision, and somewhere between three hundred fifty and four hundred, I lost the passion. When I finally peaked at five hundred twenty eight pounds, well, I lost all hope. The words remained trapped inside for more than two decades.

Today, alcohol free and two hundred fifty pounds lighter, I am ready to dream again. Holding the rediscovered chronicle of my earliest hope and dreams in my hands, I find the list has not changed too much. The dream is the same, the only difference is now...I have a story to tell.

The Gloves

"People say it gets easier; it doesn't. Others say it won't hurt as much with time, yet the pain hasn't stopped. I beam with pride, however, when people declare,

'You certainly are your mother's daughter.'

I opened up the front door yesterday and was slapped in the face with an unexpected blast of chilly autumn wind. Backing up, I went to the closet and reached up to the top shelf for a pair of gloves. I felt the soft, worn leather as I pulled them down. The minute I saw them, I knew...as I slipped them onto my hands and felt the silky fur on the inside, I knew. As I raised my hand to wipe a tear from my eye, I could smell the soft, sweet smell of her mixed with the scent of the leather.

It has been a little over two years since I lost my mother. I think about her every single day. I still reach for the phone when I have good news just as I reach for the same phone when I have a bad day. Too often, I took for granted the advice and guidance I had ready and waiting at the other end of that telephone line. Calling her was like pulling up to the gas pump to refuel when my strength and courage were running on empty. She always knew what to say and how to articulate her point with subtle finesse.

When I felt abandoned and alone, a prisoner in my home, weighing over five hundred pounds, she was one of the very few people who came to check on me almost every day. She brought healthy food, along with vitamins, books, and movies for me to occupy my time and exercise my mind. I realize, today, how much it must have hurt her to see me there, desolate and immobile in my bed.

We celebrated together when my insurance company finally approved my weight loss surgery. She rode silently beside me when we were forced to hire a car to take me to the hospital for the surgery. I was far too large to fit into the front seat of her little Ford Escort. She was the last person I saw before being wheeled into the operating room and she was right there holding my hand when I awoke in intensive care. The surgery had saved my life. It did not resolve my food addiction, but it placed a Band-Aid on a wound which would one day return to haunt me.

Together, my mother and I rediscovered the world as I quickly lost over two hundred twenty pounds, enabling me to do things and go places that had been impossible just a year earlier. I broke her heart again, however, when my addiction resurfaced six years later, and adding alcohol to the miserable mix, I regained one hundred seventy pounds. I promised her I would "fix" myself and I am thankful she lived to see my resurrection. She was the inspiration and the motivation that guided and often pushed me through my darkest days. Her faith and steadfast belief in my success led me to quit drinking and lose that one hundred seventy pounds again…the healthy way.

People say it gets easier; it doesn't. Others say it won't hurt as much with time, yet the pain hasn't stopped. I beam with pride, however, when people declare, "You certainly are your mother's daughter." I get that. Her spirit does indeed live on through me. She bestowed many gifts to me through her lifetime, among them, courage, self-determination, and tenacity, which have driven me to this brand new path that awaits me.

Today, as I boldly take the first step, I begin an exciting, unpredictable journey, and though I do not have my mother's hand to hold or her soft words to give me strength and encouragement, I do have her incredible foresight and vision to guide me. I take with me the lessons she taught and the powerful values she instilled. Yes, I walk alone in body on this forthcoming adventure, but I take comfort in knowing her spirit will laugh and dance beside me all the way.

Twilight

"The snowy, winter days of December seemed to be the hardest to endure. Around her, families celebrated the holidays in warm, cozy homes filled with Christmas, family, and tradition. Emily, however, remained in this prison chamber, struggling to recall the days of her youth."

And there came a time in her twilight years, where she found herself both lonesome and alone. Emily sat day after day in her wheelchair, her red and black checked blanket arranged across her lap. In the stillness of her room, she stared inadvertently out the window, lost in her thoughts, tortured by her memories. The tiny apartment located on the first floor of a senior assisted living building was filled with but a handful of all the "things" she had acquired through the years: a photo album, a crystal vase, a silver framed photograph of her darling Peter, and a few useless knick-knacks scattered about the silent, hollow room. *Quite a disappointment*, she concluded, after a lifetime of chasing the American dream and the almighty dollar.

The snowy, winter days of December seemed to be the hardest to endure. Around her, families celebrated the holidays in warm, cozy homes filled with Christmas, family, and tradition. Emily, however, remained in this prison chamber, struggling to recall the days of her youth. She thought she had been in love a time or two until the spring of her twenty third year, when she'd found Peter, the absolute love of her life.

They had met on campus one sunny afternoon and their lives were forever changed. He was her prince, a kind and generous companion, with whom she thought all things were possible. Peter studied English and Literature while she immersed herself in the university's business/finance program. Their love was immediate and intense and they found themselves married shortly after graduation.

Everything seemed perfect. They set off for Chicago to begin careers in their chosen fields. Peter taught English Composition at a highly regarded suburban high school while Emily joined a Fortune 500 company and began racing along the corporate fast track, headed for the top. Her personal life was put on hold, for fear of losing momentum, and all efforts were focused on her career. Things screeched to a halt, however, when quite unexpectedly, a beautiful little girl with twinkling blue eyes and hair the color of sunshine fell into their lives. Emily was forced to take some time off to love and nurture this unforeseen, yet precious gift who was named Victoria. A year had not yet passed when Emily began to feel the itch, and silently, she craved the excitement of her chosen career. Peter, dear sweet Peter, sensed her unhappiness and left his teaching job behind to care for Victoria while Emily chased her dreams.

Up before dawn, six and often seven days a week, Emily slipped silently out of the house while her little family slept. She returned late in the evening, usually after Victoria had fallen back to sleep. Peter tried to be understanding, but after years of loneliness and broken promises, his support turned to angry tolerance, and his patience to exasperation. Victoria grew up and Peter grew tired. He packed a suitcase and left Emily the day their daughter went away to college.

Emily had gone on to become CEO of her company, which resulted in a rather uneventful celebration at home—alone that evening, she toasted herself with a glass of expensive wine and a bag of stale Cheetos. She had never felt so utterly abandoned and alone, not until today.

Victoria stopped by every now and again with a coffeecake or sugar cookies from the bakery around the corner. Sometimes, she brought a bouquet of flowers which she slipped into the crystal vase where they would remain until brown and brittle, eventually crumbling to the table below. Having such a busy life, Victoria could never stay long and the visits became shorter and less frequent as time went on. Emily could not be surprised, much less angry, for this was her fate, her karma, her destiny. Victoria had learned by example, and her mentor had, of course, been her own mother, Emily.

Sitting there, alone, waiting for a stranger to roll her downstairs to the dining room, she thought of Peter and longed to see his smile. Emily picked up a silver frame from the table and stared at the old and faded photograph. She clutched it tightly to her heart and cried. She had held the greatest treasure in life for a time and carelessly let it slip away.

It was with great regret that Emily came to realize the importance of family and the value of time. The money and possessions meant nothing now, as she sat there abandoned in her solemn purgatory, where she found herself suspended between a wasted life and an eventual death. If only she had realized sooner that although time was free, time was also priceless.

Shooting Stars

"Tonight, sitting alone in her car in the twilight hours of the evening, she looked up at the stars and wondered what would become of her? What dismal fate had been predetermined for her future?"

Sitting quietly in her ancient Chevy Citation she crammed her hand between the door and the driver's seat in search of the concealed plastic lever. Yanking it up, her head bounced off the headrest as her seat jutted backward. Heaving a sigh of relief, she liberated herself from the tight space between the steering wheel and the seat. Very skillfully, she unbuttoned the top button of her size 56 jeans, causing her stomach to gush out and spill over the top of her pants.

A heavy sigh filled the car as she tore the wrapper off the last burrito in the bag and shoved it voraciously into her mouth—chomping and chewing ravenously, even though she was not really hungry anymore. An unexpected burp shot out of her mouth as the last bite made its way down to the pit of her stomach. Laying her head back, she closed her eyes, struggling to breathe while crushing the last wrapper into a ball and tossing it behind the passenger seat. It dropped to the heavily littered floor below where it joined the extensive collection of wrappers and food containers from every fast food joint within in a ten mile radius of her home.

As she sat, quite uncomfortably, waiting for the cheap, imitation Mexican feast to digest and afford her some relief, she tried to remember when this obsession with food had hijacked her life and seized her soul. She could not pinpoint an exact day or find a single person or reason to which she could place the blame. In the beginning, it had progressed at a leisurely pace. Her mind had played a pretty big part in the capture and eventual takeover.

It first convinced her it was okay to use food to return sanity and control to an overly stressful situation. Then, of course, nothing eases the pain of a bad break-up like a gallon of Rocky Road chocolate ice cream smothered in hot fudge and whipped cream. In reality, she supposed that her split from the only man she'd ever loved and their eventual divorce had thrust everything into high gear. She could not blame him for leaving, though…not really. Neither of them had bargained for the creature she had become.

In an attempt to remain positive, he had been supportive and patient with her as she bounced from one diet plan to the next while shelling out hundreds of dollars paying for the countless gym memberships that had gone ignored and unused after the first exhausting week. She'd become an expert at concocting excuses. Eventually, he stopped arguing, bargaining, and then he just stopped caring. They grew apart as their relationship fell apart, and then one day he was gone. Crushed and brokenhearted, she became a miserable recluse—a prisoner in her own home.

Feeling lost and alone, she took comfort where she could find it and found solace in food. Sleeping all day, she usually did her foraging after dark, when the rest of the world was tucked into bed, all warm and cozy with the one they loved. Pulling on her slippers and a sweatshirt, she slipped out into the night like a vampire in search of her prey. In all actuality, there was not much searching involved. It was more like choosing your quarry.

Midnight drive-thru windows became her porthole to the world. She knew the grave shift workers at every fast food place in town, and they knew her. Quite often, two, or even three stops were in order. If she could not decide between finger-licking chicken and two all-beef patties smothered in special sauce, she would solve the perplexing dilemma by buying both, making sure to get a bit extra to enjoy on the ride home. She would have her first course out of the bag, unwrapped, and on the passenger seat before she even pulled out of the driveway and made sure to finish the first bag of deep-fried delights before she pulled into her own.

Tonight, sitting alone in her car in the twilight hours of the evening, she looked up at the stars and wondered what would become of her? What dismal fate had been predetermined for her future? Was it too late to chart another course and change the direction of her life? She stared off into the heavens, reflecting, contemplating, and deliberating, when it happened.

A sudden burst of light flashed swiftly across the darkened sky. It scared her at first, forcing a gasp through her lips along with a sudden jolt of adrenaline to her heart. Suddenly, she realized it was a shooting star…but not just any star….*her* star. In her heart, she knew it was a sign…it was a symbol of hope.

Closing her eyes, she made a wish like she had never done before. She took it upon herself to be a bit greedy, just this once, and asked the powers above for not just one wish, but three. First, she prayed for the courage to begin this crucial journey toward health and happiness. Then she wished for the strength to push through the very difficult days ahead, and finally, she hoped to find the patience to allow herself all the time necessary to reach her goals.

Taking a deep breath, she looked at herself in the rearview mirror, and for the first time in a very long time, she saw hope and a smile.

The Silver Screen

"Today, you are here for redemption…a revenge of sorts. You come alone…just in case…well, just in case it happens again."

Going to the movies —it's a simple pleasure enjoyed by everyone. Who doesn't love the smell of the hot, buttered popcorn spilling into the giant, glass bins as you pass by, or the sound of squealing children anxious to see the next adventure of Harry Potter? Hidden away in their dark and dismal homes, there are a select few who have not had the delight of strolling up to the ticket window or relished in the excitement of scanning over the lighted billboard filled with this week's brand new releases. It has been a long time since they have experienced the joy of watching a movie up on the big screen.

A dark theater is a place of escape, fantasy, and whimsy, where one is transported to another place, day, or time for two hours. Most people walk through the doorway, past the black satin curtains, and head for the middle rows and the center seats...the best seats. But you are not "most" people. You're a tentative visitor, cautiously walking into the theater alone. Inching your way, slowly, toward the first available seat...you settle for one on the end. Your heart pounds as you near what has been a source of anxiety and intimidation for longer than you care to remember.

Quickly, you glance around to make sure no one is watching. They are not. Instead, they sit ripping open their giant boxes of Goobers and Sno-Caps, shoving greasy, hot popcorn into their mouths. They fiddle in their seats, checking their cell phones before the opening credits begin to roll. Pausing, you look at the red velvet seat and can remember your last visit to this same theater almost seven years ago. Squirming, you recall the embarrassment suffered that night when you attempted to squeeze yourself into that empty seat. Embarrassed, you shifted and struggled to the horrified look of your best friend who followed behind you as you fled, mortified, out of the auditorium.

Today, you are here for redemption...a revenge of sorts. You come alone...just in case...well, just in case it happens again. Hovering in front of the portentous seat, your heart pounding in your ears, you take a deep breath, close your eyes, and sit.

To your pleasant surprise, you glide easily into the seat as you exhale madly. The tears well in your eyes as the big, beautiful screen transforms into a kaleidoscope of Technicolor. Settling back into your chair as the movie begins, you smile, and knowing inside you will remember this movie for the rest of your life. The great adventure of the day was finding the courage to walk into the building....the movie...whatever it is...is just a bonus.

Fireworks

But "sensible" was not sensational.

And then it happened...

No cautionary forewarning ...not even a simple suspicion. It was a day like so many other average days. She had settled into the notion of just plain settling. There would never be skyrockets or fireworks. Following the distress of her last broken heart, she had astutely convinced herself that dependable and reliable were honest traits. Knowing you had someone responsible to lean on was best....for her and her son. Fireworks were overrated, anyway. She descended into a relationship of convenience, deciding that being lonely was better than being alone. Was she even worthy of love or happiness? Being a woman of a "particular" age prompts one to consider their options and then procure the most sensible choice.

But "sensible" was not sensational. It was not magnificent or amazing or superb. Sensible was monotonous, flavorless, and inane. However, she had vowed to make it work for her. And then one afternoon, on an ordinary day, something extraordinary happened which tossed all sensibility out the window. She had come upon an unexpected stranger.

When their eyes met she could feel the blood rush to her face. For an unforeseen moment, she lost her breath...and then felt a strange quivering in her heart. Frightened and confused, she attempted to disregard the sudden sense of lightheadedness which had so enthusiastically seized her soul. She could not remember ever experiencing such an occurrence. She took a deep breath, smiled, and took the first step of a journey that would define and transform her existence. Suddenly, dependable wasn't nearly enough to ignore the possibility of "incredibly remarkable." Besides, it was nearly July and the promise of a few fireworks in her future was more than enough to justify the journey.

The Piano

"They do not grasp the emotional devastation of it all, but they will one day...they will, for they, too, are growing up and like it or not, they, too, are growing old"

Emily sits there alone, next to the shiny black piano, locked inside her own mind. Her eyes stare at the keys, scarcely blinking, while her hands rest motionless upon her lap. Her calcified fingers lay there, inert, perpetually curled and virtually useless. These are the same fingers that once danced across the keys, pounding out symphonies by Ludwig van Beethoven and concertos written by Mozart and Tchaikovsky.

Whenever she played, she was one with the music. Every note coursed through her veins as her heart beat in rhythm with the melody. She had been blessed with an amazing talent which had afforded her the opportunity to travel the world. She'd played for sophisticated audiences in Paris and Berlin, London and New York City; but that was oh so long ago. Things were different now.

Today, just like every other day, her wheelchair is rolled up next to the beautiful old piano, which sits, as she does, silenced and ignored in the corner of the room. They leave her there, alone for hours, as they rush around to complete their daily tasks. The torture of being so close, yet so far away from her treasured friend is almost too hard to bear.

Though she sits motionless, she still remembers. Nostalgically, she remembers the feeling of her fingers gliding across the ivory colored keys, heart racing as her feet pumped the pedals beneath the magnificent baby grand piano. She pictured herself in perfect posture, as she was a stunning young lady with scarlet red hair and emerald green eyes which danced back and forth across the brittle, yellowed scores of music.

The sheets of composition were there but for appearances only, for she knew every bar, every rest, and every note by heart. The young do not understand the longing of the old. There is no comprehension of life slipping away and no consideration for why the aged try so hard to hang on to the little things they have left in life; a photograph, a locket, or maybe a simple teacup.

They do not grasp the emotional devastation of it all, but they will one day…they will, for they, too, are growing up and like it or not, they, too, are growing old. Their music, like Emily's, will one day fade away and they will find themselves being wheeled around like a piece of furniture—talked about but never spoken to.

For Emily, the music still plays in her mind with every imagined crescendo crushing the unbearable silence which suffocates her soul. Oh, how her hands beg and plead with her mind to allow her to touch the keys once more. Her heart aches to make the music come alive again. If only she could hear the thunderous applause overpower an electrified auditorium just one more time. She would have appreciated that final concert so much more, had she only known. The trouble is, you never realize it is the last time ...until it is.

Smile

"I knew I would need to change...heck, who was I kidding? It would take a transformation of massive proportions to prove my devotion."

I awoke one day and found you gone. One can never prepare themselves for such a loss. It was extreme, profound, and overwhelming. Sure, I know that I took you for granted. I ignored the telltale signs. I pretended not to notice that our time together began to diminish and your show of affection had ceased to exist. Good friends and family tried to warn me of your intention to leave…but my pride and stubborn attitude refused to listen.

And then it happened. I looked around, and you were gone. I searched for you like a mad woman. I grew hopeless and discouraged as the loss began to sink in. Sitting alone, desolate and defeated, I had to wonder: what would I do without you, and where would I be without my smile?

The days slipped past and the nights dragged on while the clock continued to keep track of each and every lonely hour spent apart. I told myself and those who asked that I was fine without you. I did not miss you, for what did I have to smile about, anyway? When you find yourself alone, female, fat, and fifty, there really isn't much to smile about, now is there?

Still, truth be told, I did miss you, immensely. Days were sad and melancholy without you, your joy…your laughter. I began to hope for your return, and then I began to consider how I could make that happen. I thought perhaps the promise of change might lure you in and then I realized it would take far more than a host of empty promises to bring you home. I knew I would need to change…heck, who was I kidding? It would take a transformation of massive proportions to prove my devotion. And with that, an idea became my reality.

I started eating healthy and working out, walking, and attending meetings. I became accountable for what I did and all I ate. I watched and waited for you to appear…and I waited and waited…and waited. I became obsessed with counting. Counting steps, counting calories, and eventually, I began to count my blessings. As days passed, I watched the transformation occur.

My body began to shrink and my self-confidence began to grow. The negativity disappeared as my future brightened.

And then one day, the magic happened. I stepped upon the scale after nearly a year of devoted dedication. My heart began to race as the blood rushed to my head. I felt excited, proud, and almost giddy as I took a moment to comprehend the fact *I had lost a hundred pounds*. My chest swelled and my heart raced as I steadied myself on the scale. I slowly looked into the mirror…and there you were, in all your glory. You were right there looking back at me…my smile had returned.

Free

And then it happens. Serendipity steps in. Call it fate, chance or kismet, the definition is irrelevant."

There comes a day in every relationship that will define future of its existence. One of you will begin to wonder if this is how you envisioned your life. You will consider the past and speculate about the future and quite possibly, after much time and consideration, your heart will whisper…no. You will sit alone in perfect silence and begin to ponder a life without your current lover, and because it is easier to not think so hard about something so painful, you will shake your head and try to push aside those notions.

As time passes, you rationalize the opinion that while things weren't perfect, they could be worse. This logic will suffice for the moment and you will carry on, ignoring the growing feeling of trepidation which looms in the recesses of your mind. Alone, you defend and validate your shrinking list of reasons to stay, yet your mind questions this whole process of justification.

And then it happens. Serendipity steps in. Call it fate, chance or kismet, the definition is irrelevant. What matters is the fact that something much bigger than your fear, conscience, or self-imposed virtue takes over and for some unexplained reason you let it.

The meeting occurred quite by chance. The conversation was effortless, spontaneous, and easy. The spark was unexpected... delightful, refreshing, and instantly they both knew that destiny was at work and the future of this wonderful connection would be left in the hands of a much greater power than either of them could begin to imagine.

You question daily the sudden magic of something so new and unfamiliar. The genuineness of the determined advances made by a thrilling stranger come into question, and while your head says *relax, slow down*, your heart dances inside of your chest at the ring of a telephone or the arrival of a letter.

Suddenly, the decision you have considered for so long seems unavoidable, inevitable, even unstoppable. Your heart, mind, and soul become one and give you the permission to enjoy the electrifying exhilaration of exploring this unexpected romance.

It is with great sadness you realize that following this dream will involve the closure of another, and while it will bruise your heart, it will also exhilarate your soul. Somehow you will recognize and accept the fact that this temporary pain will clear the way for a lifetime of unbelievable bliss and happiness.

Tossing caution to the wind, you step out of the simple life you have been living, straight into the adventure of a lifetime and at that single moment you feel free.

The Warrior

Go ahead...knock me over. Kick me when I'm down,

Just realize, that when you are done I will get up.

I always, always, always get back up; and when I do

I will be faster, stronger, smarter and ready for anything.

Go ahead and laugh at my misfortune or my failures.

Unlike you, I have learned that one cannot

Appreciate the magnificence of winning

Until you have been brought to your knees by losing.

I have been at the top of the world

Only to find myself in a free fall,

Spiraling quickly downward to the ground.

I have learned humility and tasted sweet success.

Believe me....success is better.

So, my friend, do your best to defeat me.

Just keep in mind you played a huge part

In teaching me how to do battle.

I have watched and learned from the master.

The worst mistake you ever made, was teaching me...

How to beat you at your own game.

Going In Means Coming Out

"It was as if something were trying to keep me from getting out and venturing into the mysterious, unknown world hidden behind that single, unremarkable door."

I sat there, staring intently through the cracked windshield of my old 1987 Pontiac Catalina. Gigantic raindrops fell from the evening sky, splattering on the roof of the car like massive water balloons. The clouds had opened suddenly with this torrential downpour just as I was about to make my way across the parking lot. It was as if something were trying to keep me from getting out and venturing into the mysterious, unknown world hidden behind that single, unremarkable door. It forced me to sit and reconsider the necessity of this not so accidental escapade.

I looked intently at the front of this ordinary looking cinder block building. It was a bar, a simple little corner bar. The faded rainbow flag draped across the inside of the front window was the only thing that announced its "open gayness" to the outside world. To me, it represented a "welcome home" banner of sorts, even though I had never set foot in the place before. Yes, I had driven past many times, and I had even stopped and parked a time or two, here in this very spot.

Afraid of the unknown, I had become an inconspicuous voyeur—watching, wondering and waiting—although, just exactly what I continued waiting for was unclear. A sign, an invitation, or perhaps divine intervention may have been my expectation. At any rate, I received none, and yet, there I sat, staring at the worn and battered wooden door.

On this rainy night, something felt different, unusual. Today was the day, I could feel it. The courage peaked within me just as lighting ripped across the murky August sky. Slipping the keys out of the ignition, I took a deep breath, and pushed the Pontiac's door open. Tonight, I would find the strength to leave the security of my own sheltered world, face my fears, and pass through that menacing doorway. Realizing at that very instant, there really was no choice — the only way for me to ever "come out" was to actually go in — so I slammed the door and made my way across the parking lot as raindrops fell on my face.

The Bird

"She begged her captor to let her go....to set her free, and give her a chance to even, just once again, spread her tattered wings in the sunshine"

There she was, a magnificent bird soaring high above us all, so proud and radiant, with her head held high and her feathers beautiful and bright. Content to live alone, she shared only her glorious song with the world below. One day, a net was cast upon her. Terrified, she thrashed about, trying furiously to escape; regrettably she could not and was taken away from her forest sanctuary and forced into a cage where she spent countless days and immeasurable hours longing for her freedom.

Her captor tried to keep her content and give her all the things he thought she wanted. Unable to comprehend why the tiny bird was so unhappy, he spent much time with the bird, encouraging her to sing and enjoy life. The bird began to look forward to time spent with her keeper, in fact, she found herself developing a deep love for him. However, she still craved flight and the former life she'd left behind. In her sadness, her song became joyless and melancholy instead. Her once bright and illustrious coat of feathers turned dull and gradually fell from her wings to lay forsaken upon the bottom of her prison.

Eventually, her jailer grew tired of her despair and loathsome appearance and returned home with a new bird. The new bird was brighter and younger and seemed full of life and the first bird's heart was shattered. She begged her captor to let her go....to set her free, and give her a chance to even, just once again, spread her tattered wings in the sunshine. Reluctantly, he opened the door of the cage for her to leave; however, she could barely walk...let alone fly. He gently picked her up and carried her outside and back to the tree where he had discovered her.

He placed her on a branch and she began to sing...barely audible at first, but each note gave her strength and the power to go on. Every day became relaxed and easier and today, in fact, if you walk past that tree you will hear a song so rich and beautiful that you might be tempted to make it your own. Keep walking, though. The bird sings for herself now.

The Last Word

"There were melancholy days when I missed her so much it was hard to function. I sat and recalled sitting beside her, holding her frail hand as she struggled to take her final breath."

Waking from a restless slumber, I noticed the clock on the nightstand declared three am. Wide awake, I lay there in the darkness for a few minutes, unable to go back to sleep. Kicking off the covers, I slid my feet into my slippers and padded my way through the dark house. My two sleepy Chihuahuas sat up, yawning and wondering what all the fuss was about. Reluctantly, they stretched, jumped off the bed, and fell in step behind me as we proceeded down the hallway.

By intuition, my feet led me quite naturally to the kitchen and slid their way in silence across the tiled floor to stop directly in front of the grand, double door refrigerator. My hand rested upon the handle, and out of habit and without a second thought, the door opened and light flooded the darkened room. If there had been a chorus of angels in the vicinity, they would have belted out a note in unison at that precise moment.

Standing there, blinking the sleep from my eyes, I stared vacantly at the wealth of food stored within. Taking a breath, and then heaving a sigh, I stepped back and closed the door. Abruptly, I turned and headed into the living room, where I slid the glass patio door open and stepped out onto the deck into the chilly night air. Wrapping my arms around myself, I looked up into the sky. The dogs poked their heads out and decided to scamper back to the warmth of the bed. Above me, a blanket of stars twinkled brilliantly and the moon bathed my yard in a ghostly, silver glow.

Sitting down on the porch swing, I relaxed and enjoyed the pleasant silence. Suddenly, I realized I had been dreaming about my mother again. There were melancholy days when I missed her so much it was hard to function. I sat and recalled sitting beside her, holding her frail hand as she struggled to take her final breath. She had, without a doubt, been my closest and dearest friend, constant cheerleader, and harshest critic.

My mom had suffered right along with me during my food addiction. I am sure it broke her heart to see me reach the five hundred pound mark. She was there when I hit my rock bottom and thankfully lived to see me scratch and crawl my way out of that bottomless hole, offering me tough love and encouragement the whole way.

I remember finding a little pink pig on my kitchen windowsill one day after she had left my home. Hanging around its neck was a little sign that stated quite simply, "No More Pigging Out." I did not speak to her for ten days after finding that little pig. I smiled to myself and stood up, deciding a ham sandwich might just help me erase the sad memories and go back to sleep.

I stepped back into the warm house and made my way to the kitchen. I pulled an armload of goodies out of the refrigerator and placed the pile of food on the counter next to the kitchen sink. As I turned on the faucet to wash my hands, I noticed a peculiar little pig staring at me. It had sat there on the windowsill for the better part of a year and had gone unnoticed until today...right this very minute. I studied the little figurine for quite some time before looking up and seeing my reflection staring back at me in the kitchen window.

I stood there with the water running and thought to myself, *What are you doing? Why would you eat all of this food at three in the morning?* I turned off the water, and as I loaded the food back into the refrigerator, I glanced at the pig and read out loud, "No More Pigging Out." With that, I shuffled back to my cozy little bedroom, and as I climbed underneath the worn and weathered quilt, I thought to myself, *Well, there you go again, Mother...always getting the last word!*

Regret

"Day by day, I watched as my world became smaller and smaller while I became bigger and bigger. I really felt the world closing in on me as I slowly began to accept the fact I probably wouldn't be around long enough to grow old."

I have spent too many days of my life saying no and things like… I can't….I won't…and I have never. In doing this, I have missed out on so many things which would have enriched my life and made me whole. I was afraid to try so many things because of my fears and insecurities.

Yes, a year ago—and for many years before that—things were much more difficult. I was stumbling through life with "a dead body" on my back. Everything I did was difficult. To walk to my car was a chore. Day by day, I watched as my world became smaller and smaller while I became bigger and bigger. I really felt the world closing in on me as I slowly began to accept the fact I probably wouldn't be around long enough to grow old. Even the few things that gave me hope in my life slipped away…and I stood by and let them go.

I did not feel like I deserved to be happy and worked hard at making myself and those around me miserable. I built a wall and pushed away those I loved and shut out a couple of beautiful souls, either of which I could have built a real life with. Instead, I found myself in a "relationship" with food and alcohol…neither of which had any love for me.

I awoke one day at four in the afternoon after a weekend of binging on junk food and drowning my senses in alcohol, and it all hit me. I lay there and cried until not a single teardrop was left. That was the day I decided to take my life back. I spent the bulk of that year learning discipline and restraint. I began this incessant journey by giving up and letting go (something I had already proven myself to be quite good at) only this time, I let go of the things that were stealing my life.

Today, almost three years later, I find myself at a different place. It is a place of hope and promise. Every single day I feel stronger, healthier, and more ALIVE. Every pound I shed gives me greater freedom…the freedom to stop saying no and instead scream out yes…Yes…YES! Every day I try something new, go somewhere I have never gone, and say yes to something I would not have even "been able" to do just one short year ago.

I am not going to sit and watch life pass me by, sitting in a chair with a twenty-five-year-old spirit imprisoned inside of an eighty-year-old body. I intend to start living my bucket list now, today. There are regrets I have for things I did or DID NOT do in my past. I have realized it is not too late to make things right. I know what I want and where I am going. I am not afraid anymore. The only regret I will have in my life is my remorse for a life that was half over before it ever began.

The Carnival

"Walking back down the up-ramp with her head down in shame, she had struggled to hide her crimson cheeks from the other cruel and laughing children."

Her foot slipped back and forth rapidly from the accelerator to the brake pedal. Traffic was maddening on Friday afternoons, especially as the final days of the summer season drew near. Everyone struggled to squeeze in all of the things they had planned and intended to accomplish before Labor Day. Now, here they were, with the unfinished list still looming, celebrating the final weekend of summer. This had been an eventful year for her; in fact, she had accomplished more this summer than she had in the past two decades combined.

To say she had come out of her shell would be a reasonable description, though maybe a bit modest. Recently, she had liberated herself from the self-imposed prison which had stifled her life for far too long. After losing well over two hundred pounds, she'd experienced a reincarnation of sorts, a reawakening, a rebirth. It had been a prolonged and lengthy process, which she realized was ongoing. It had taken her many years to feel strong enough to face the world once again.

Of course, she had not crossed the finish line by any means, but she was back in the race, where even last place was exhilarating. With great enthusiasm, she felt her mind and spirit growing stronger, ever expanding, as her body reduced and condensed itself. Recently, she had considered the notion that she might have discovered the fountain of youth somewhere along the journey, for she felt younger and more invigorated as days slipped by. Unreservedly, she began traveling to places and doing things she had not even considered just a short time ago and this made her feel vibrant and alive!

As the little car crept along in rush hour traffic, she twisted the air conditioning knob once again, which still did absolutely nothing. The sun beat down on her through the windshield, making her feel like a bug under a magnifying glass and she realized she needed out of the scorching hot car, at least until this five o'clock rush hour absurdity had subsided. Looking ahead, she noticed the colorful flags rippling in the wind. A blue and yellow Ferris wheel rolled lazily in the sky. "A carnival," she thought out loud, and without hesitation, she yanked the steering wheel to the right and skidded across the gravel into the busy parking lot as horns blared and blasted behind her. Not having ventured through the gates of a carnival since she was a young girl, she hesitated but the kid deep inside her whispered, "Today is the day."

As she sauntered past the "Mid-American Midway" ticket booth, a flirtatious concoction of delightful scents and smells engulfed her entire being. Hot, buttered popcorn mixed with warm, sticky cotton candy and foot-long hotdogs simmering on the grill overwhelmed her senses and it took great restraint and control to stroll past the enthusiastic vendors without stopping to sample any of the tempting treats. She had spent three years preparing for this battle and moved along with confidence.

She had forgotten how overwhelming the magical world of the midway was. The numerous sights, sounds, and smells overloaded one's senses. The peculiar music from the various rides and attractions traversed upon the muggy air in an eerie drone, sounding much like a warped record playing on a very old phonograph machine.

She stood and watched the white horses of the carousel bob up and down while the children riding pompously upon them squealed in delight. As she worked her way toward the center of the tiny self-contained community, she came upon the games of chance. "All down...all ready....all ready...all down," the carnival barker yelled out to his customers who were frantically placing bets on their favorite colors as he reached up to spin the giant wheel of chance. In the booth next to him, children tossed small wooden rings at longneck pop bottles...the sound of *tink...tink...tink* filled the air as the rings continuously bounced off the bottles, provoking the disappointed tykes to shell out yet another torn and tattered dollar bill in hopes of winning a stuffed teddy bear.

As she stood and watched, temptation once again crept upon her. *Elephant ears, deep fried Oreos, and Funnel cakes*, the bright neon sign exclaimed! She did not need a sign to attract her attention. She recognized this sweet temptation long before the blinking billboard ever came into view. The intoxicating aroma made her head swim and she decided it might be best to turn and head in a different direction before this mounting craving got the best of her.

Behind her, she heard the distinct, unmistakable

click...click...click of an ancient roller coaster straining to ascend the highest peak of the track. Glancing over her shoulder, she turned just in time to see the "Dizzy Dragon" climb up and over the hill, rushing rapidly down the other side as little hands flew up into the air and riders gasped and screamed in joyful terror! In a fleeting moment of recollection, she smiled, remembering the roller coaster had been her favorite ride as child and even a young adult...until she had grown too large to lower the safety bar over her protruding belly.

Spinning on her heel, she turned and began moving once again. Strolling past the Funhouse and a wild spinning ride called The Vertigo, she glanced up and found herself directly in front of the towering Ferris wheel. Using her hand to shade the sun from her eyes, she stared up at the twenty or so bucket seats rocking empty in the wind and thought how exhilarating and free it must feel to tower above the earth.

Any and all hopes to board this type of amusement ride had long been abandoned since the afternoon she had been forced to climb out of the constricted roller coaster seat for being too "large" for the ride. Walking back down the up-ramp with her head down in shame, she had struggled to hide her crimson cheeks from the other cruel and laughing children.

With her heart racing, she looked up once more and then strolled over to the little red and white striped ticket booth, handing the woman a five dollar bill. "Just one," she stated with a tiny quiver in her voice. Grabbing the ticket and her change, she headed back to the giant spinning wheel. The grubby looking carnie smiled at her and she could not help but notice the vacant spot in his grin where his front tooth had been. Hesitantly, she smiled back as he took the ticket and led her up the shaking metal ramp.

As she stepped up into the bucket, she took a deep breath while politely ignoring the greasy outstretched hand extended to help her. As she sat down on the hot vinyl seat, she felt her heart stop beating as the carnie reached up to close the safety bar and exhaled uncontrollably as the bar snapped easily into place. Relieved, and thankful, she sat up straight and rested her arm across the back of the gently swaying seat.

As the magnificent machine jerked into motion, her heart swelled in gratitude and appreciation for this second chance at life she had so graciously been granted.

As she reached what felt like the top of the world, she beamed an enormous smile. Looking out through the shimmering heatwaves, she could see the flourishing city for miles around. "The world is mine," she whispered under her breath, and raised her hands above her, laughing uncontrollably as she headed back down.

What do I Value?

"You can save, spend, and lose a fortune, only to win the lottery the next day, but time is fleeting. Precious days, hours, and even seconds are stolen from us, never to be returned."

What do I value most in life? The answer changes from day to day. Three years ago, almost to the day, as my mother lay dying in a hospital bed, I most valued the time I had left with her. I savored every second, hung on to every word, and tried to etch every smile into my memory. A year later, I place value in each and every lesson my mother taught me. I value the strength and independence she passed on to both my sister and myself. I finally recognize the sacrifices she made to give us a better life. I have come to understand and appreciate the many lessons she instilled in us, although, at the time, her words seemed to fall upon deaf ears.

I now realize time is so much more valuable than money. You can save, spend, and lose a fortune, only to win the lottery the next day, but time is fleeting. Precious days, hours, and even seconds are stolen from us, never to be returned. Think of all you can see, hear, and smell in just an hour of walking through a forest. The sunsets, snowflakes, and wildflowers we take for granted every day as we rush to our cars, late for work. The smiles, hugs, and handshakes we sacrifice in a world focused on texting and typing.

Think about all the real friendships lost in place of our "social networks." They are replaced, instead, with a ten-year-old picture of someone we will never meet, who can only offer an invitation to play "Candy Crush" in return for your so called friendship.

What do I value, you ask? I place immeasurable

worth on loyalty, honesty, and integrity. I have been deceived, misled, and betrayed throughout my lifetime. I have placed my trust in some loathsome individuals who did not understand the priceless gift they had been given. They took my kindness as weakness and preyed upon my good nature. The scars they left upon my heart and soul were hurtful and disheartening, but the lessons learned were significant and invaluable.

I was forced to examine my life and to learn to appreciate my true friends. Today, I realize that the sincere devotion of just one friend means more than the artificial admiration of a dozen. A true friend, I have found, will tell you when you're wrong...to your face...and not behind your back.

I value my education and am thankful for the opportunity I have been given to go back to school and use my brain! I value the lessons taught by my mentors and instructors along with each and every personal experience they share with me. Learning is living. To stop learning is to begin dying.

So, as I said, the things I value may change a bit from day to day. Often, one doesn't realize how valuable something really is until it is forever lost. Today, I must say, that I value most, the expectation I will wake up tomorrow and use that time to do something I have never done, see something I have never seen, and accomplish something I have never even imagined.

To See It Coming

"Admit it or don't, but you did see it approaching. It sped toward you like a freight train on a track."

Staring at your unrecognizable impression in the mirror, you will swear to all that you never saw it coming and you have absolutely no idea how or when you ballooned up to five hundred pounds. Obviously, you knew things were a bit out of control when your pants size whizzed through the "portly" forties and settled into the hefty fifties, but at thirty-five years old, you never thought that you would find yourself lying stretched out on your bed, struggling to zip up a pair of size 66 jeans.

Wow, how did that happen, and with that being the largest size you could find anywhere...what would you do now?

Admit it or don't, but you *did* see it approaching. It sped toward you like a freight train on a track. In an effort to forget, you shove from your mind any recollection of the nights you pulled through Taco Bell and ordered $20 worth of burritos, on your way to pick up the pizza you were having for dinner with your roommate. Quite conveniently, you lost count of the hundreds and probably thousands of Quarter pounders with cheese you shoveled through your mouth, every single day, as if you might never eat again. It was an addiction, a compulsion, an obsession with food. Your body craved its food fix as bad as any junkie might hunger for their own drug of choice, or worse, necessity.

Perhaps, you should have realized it Halloween night as you ate yourself into a sugar coma—devouring the candy you bought to hand out to the trick or treaters. Open bags of fun-size Snicker bars, Reese's Cups, M&Ms, and Milky Ways surrounded you on the sofa, while wrappers and empty plastic bags lay at your feet upon the floor. Just like last Halloween, you convinced yourself you would need at least a dozen bags of candy, even though you had only seen a dozen little witches and zombies at your door last year. In the back of your mind, you realized that choosing all of your favorites would make the leftovers go down much quicker. Impatiently, you'd turned the porch light off after just five or six groups of children bellowed "Trick or Treat" at your front door. Sitting there in the darkness with only the television on, you munched madly on the piles of candy and cringed every time you heard children pass the house.

Oh yeah, the signs were there, screaming at you. You could see your eyes pleading with yourself in the mirror each time you washed your hands or brushed your teeth. Your knees cried out whenever you struggled to your feet. Your heart strained and battled to beat in a consistent cadence while your lungs wheezed and gasped for air. There is no denying the ghastly reality of your disorder or the unmistakable circumstances that nearly led to your demise. Denial is a coping skill, however, not a skill one can ever brag about.

Facing this aggressive demon is difficult, in part, because the world is not sympathetic to your plight. "Why can't you just go on a diet?" they shout or "Get up and exercise! You're just being lazy!" is another bit of "skinny people" wisdom. The truth of the matter is this: If you find yourself growing out of your clothes or furniture, you have a problem. When your weight begins to control every facet of your life, you must get help.

You will not do it on your own. *You need the support of a group such as Weight Watchers to espouse and encourage you.* If you reach the morbidly obese status, you must get professional help. It will not go away on its own. This addiction will devour your soul and leave you sick, hopeless, and alone if it doesn't steal your actual life first.

Believe me when I tell you there is hope and promise. You have it within you to do battle with this addiction. Weighing five hundred twenty eight pounds myself, I had weight loss surgery fourteen years ago, lost more than two hundred pounds, and then gained most of it back. So while the surgery had indeed saved my life, it was not a lifetime solution. The root of this severe addiction was never acknowledged or addressed, and therefore never resolved.

For three years now, I have battled for my life, fighting this monster every single day. The good news is that I am winning, having lost two hundred fifty pounds through hard work, Weight Watchers support, and counseling. There is a bit of a journey left ahead of me, but I say with confidence that I have my life back!

There was a time when I could not wait to fall asleep at night. I would dwell in heavy slumber as long as possible, for these midnight dreams were my only escape from the solemn reality which was my life. These days, I climb into bed late and open my eyes to watch the sunrise outside my window. I appreciate the realization that I am healing and on my way to a full recovery, because suddenly, an ordinary day… is better than an extraordinary dream.

The Mighty Oak

"Staring out of the tiny window into the peaceful forest, she smiled and felt safe, happy, and content. She thanked the tree and wrapped her arms around its massive trunk."

There was a young girl who longed for a place she could call her own. One day, she decided to build a tree house; something simple, in a quiet spot where she could relax and be herself. Determined, she ventured off into the woods and found the perfect tree. Leaning upon the mighty oak, she looked up and asked, "May I borrow one of your branches to construct a little tree house?"

The lonely old tree, excited to have some company whispered, "Why yes...yes! Please do!" She started building right away, using whatever she could find to construct the house. The new getaway didn't have to be perfect. After all, it wasn't forever; just a place where she could hide until the autumn leaves turned brown. After many long hours of hard work, she finally collapsed into the corner of her new little sanctuary.

Staring out of the tiny window into the peaceful forest, she smiled and felt safe, happy, and content. She thanked the tree and wrapped her arms around its massive trunk. The tree stood proud and happy to have found a purpose...and a friend. As the days passed, the little girl found herself adding more and more to her once simple structure. Furniture, books, clothes, and soon she ran out of room for all of the "stuff". The tree quietly suggested that perhaps she should not add anymore to the structure. It hinted that maybe it was time to find a younger, stronger tree? She ignored the tree's requests and added yet another room.

She crammed in still more...and more of her belongings. Beneath her, the branches proceeded to bend and creak from the added stress of so much baggage. She tried to reinforce the fortress with sticks and anything else she could find, and yet the branch continued to sag and the tree silently moaned. The girl became irritated at first, and then angry at the tree for not being stronger and supporting her house. Eventually, the branch snapped and the girl and everything around her tumbled to the ground.

"I hate you," screamed the girl as she stormed off out of the woods, never to return again. With its roots winding into the ground below, the tree could not go after the girl. Standing there sadly, with its leaves turning brown, the once mighty oak raised its branches to the cold, gray sky and stood alone and broken in the forest.

Under the Stars

Be brave…be courageous…be fearless and fly

My eyes snapped open at daybreak. The symphony of sparrows, blue jays, and robins filled the air with a lonesome whippoorwill keeping time in the background. It took a moment to adjust to my surroundings, when suddenly I realized that today...this very day...was my birthday.

I smiled as I sat up in the peculiar and unfamiliar environment of the little camper. That's when it all came back to me...I had done it! I had ventured from my safe and sheltered circle of my traditional reality! It had taken all the courage that I could muster to break my routine and embark on this little adventure, but here I was breathing in the crisp, clear air and enjoying the calming scent of vegetation and pine.

Twenty years of confinement in a body that had held me captive created quite a bit of anxiety and angst in regards to conquering the unknown. Camping sounds like a very "tame" venture to most people; however, when one weighs over five hundred pounds, just getting dressed in the morning to go out and check the mail is an adventure! In my skeptical mind, camping was a nightmare waiting to happen!

My brain raced with so many potential hazards and pitfalls. To begin...how do I get up the stairs into the trailer? Will the stairs hold me? And what happens when I get inside? Can you even fit into the telephone booth sized bathroom...and the shower...well, forget the shower ...once you get in, there's no getting out! Sitting around the campfire sounds quaint and charming until the legs give out on your chair, rolling you into the flames, catching your hair on fire. These are perpetual burdens and concerns faced by portly people. We become so accustomed to NOT fitting in that we grow to accept it.

This year, I chose to fight that submission. I battled my anxiety and struggled through the sudden panic I experienced upon driving through the Camp gates. Sure, I had lost two hundred fifty pounds...but in my head, I was still that five hundred pound recluse who had been disappointed so many times.

Last weekend, I chose to break free from my stifling comfort zone. I walked up to the menacing little trailer, took a deep breath, and stepped up into my little home away from home with ease. Showering every morning wasn't painful at all, after which I got dressed, and even sported a pair of shorts for the first time in thirty years. The supreme recollection of the weekend was an evening spent under a twinkling blanket of stars with a delightful collection of enthusiastic, impressive, remarkable women, who just like myself, were there to conquer their own demons. We sat around a crackling campfire and told stories until late into the night.

Each day, I walked and explored the grounds, and quite by accident, I came upon the most amazing one-hundred-year-old tree, standing proud and strong, next to a bubbling stream. The place...the moment...the experience left me breathless. Ignoring my fears, I'd taken a chance—driven up north and ventured into the forest in search of a birthday celebration many would consider insignificant and trivial.

I am delighted to say I left with a memory that will last a lifetime. To all of you reading this alone, in your bed, afraid of what is lurking outside of your home…be brave…be courageous…be fearless and fly.

The Red Balloons

A polka dot dress and her favorite red hat,
Such a beautiful child.
Curly brown hair and milky brown eyes
A daddy's girl, that's for sure,
And no one would ever deny it.
Walking through the park,
One sunny afternoon,
They came upon a vendor,
With a bunch of red balloons.
Her eyes grew wide and then she sighed
"Oh Daddy, I must have two!"
He smiled and nodded to the man
As he pulled them from the bunch.
There'd be nothing else bought the rest of the day
Or they wouldn't have enough money for lunch.
Then suddenly she decided,
That two would not suffice.
She raised the stakes,
Turned on the charm,
And then she rolled the dice.
"Oh Daddy, please, I want them ALL!
I'll ask for nothing more.
He looked at her embarrassed
And sternly told her no!
The anger boiled inside her.
A tear slipped from her eye.
She stomped her foot, crossed her arms
And then began to cry.
Right then and there he saw it coming,
Bracing for the fight,

He put his hands upon his hips
And said, "No, dear, not tonight."
The sound of the scream was piercing.
It echoed through the air.
The vendor's eyes went wide with fright
And everyone stopped to stare.
Ashamed and quite embarrassed,
He pulled out all his cash,
He wadded it up, stuck it in the cup,
And reached out his calloused right hand.
There must have been several dozen of those shiny red balloons,
Her crocodile tears stopped falling,
And her smile returned all too soon.
"Thank you, Daddy," she crooned so sweetly,
"You're welcome," he said with a sigh,
He bent over slightly, and very politely
He let them all float to the sky.

The Flying Duck Bar

*"It's like a diabetic buying a candy store!" my mother had
exclaimed to anyone who would listen."*

The old school bus lurched and lunged its way down M-65, liberating wild and crazy children at every stop. Ours was next, and I couldn't wait to leap from my seat. Before even the bus had stopped rolling, I was making my way toward the door.

"Stay sittin' down until we come to a complete stop!" Mrs. Phillips bellowed from the driver's seat.

"Sorry ma'am," I stated as I grabbed my sister's hand. We waited for her to crank the door open, and then we cleared the two steps in one giant leap and landed on the gravel shoulder of the road, right next to the rusted tin mailbox. I reached inside to grab the pile of letters and sale papers and stuffed them into my book bag as the yellow bus pulled away, leaving us standing in a cloud of rich, black exhaust fumes.

We ran to the back door of the big, obnoxious, parrot green building. We were excited because it was Friday and we had the entire weekend to do as we pleased. As I threw open the old screen door, our dog Sally, a beautiful German Shepard /Collie mix, jumped up and down in a frenzy. We gave her a quick hug and a pat on the head and then we skipped down the long hallway and up the stairs to our bedrooms with Sally's nails clicking behind us.

As we climbed, I counted....seventeen steps dragging our book bags up and seventeen steps down, lugging our laundry baskets behind us. The last four stairs up always felt like quicksand and left me panting when I reached the top. Always seventeen stairs, and yet I still counted them, every day, every time, going up and coming down.

The Flying Duck Bar flickered on the weather worn plastic sign out front. We had moved to this quiet little farming town shortly after the Detroit riot of 1967. My parents, enjoying the spoils from a long awaited injury lawsuit, decided it would be our only chance to get away from the crime and desperation of the dying city. Together, they had spent sleepless nights trying to decide which course to take, and which direction our lives should go. My father, however, had ideas of his own and without consulting my mother, signed a deal to purchase an old and failing tavern in the small town of Posen, Michigan, population 408. That unexpected purchase almost resulted in a divorce for my parents that summer. It did eventually cause their split; it just took four more years for that to happen.

"It's like a diabetic buying a candy store!" my mother had exclaimed to anyone who would listen. She had been dead set against the Flying Duck from the start, due mostly to the fact that my father had a fondness for Stroh's beer, matched only by his addiction to Viceroy Cigarettes. "It's a recipe for disaster," I'd overheard her telling Aunt Pat on the telephone. Like it or not, the deal was done, the papers signed and here we were, two years later, struggling to keep the bar, their marriage, and our crazy little family together.

On this day, though, all seemed right in the world. I headed into the bar through a door which led from the hallway through a dimly lit stockroom overflowing with cases of Black Label, Pabst Blue Ribbon, Old Milwaukee, and of course, dad's favorite, Stroh's-Bohemian Style beer. Along the back wall were half full cases of empty cans and bottles. They gave off the bitter aroma of sour beer. I always scrambled through the room, holding my breath like an Olympic swimmer, rushing to burst through the second door and into the bar itself. It wasn't much better when I gulped in the air on the other side.

Overwhelmed by the pungent stench of stale cigarette smoke, I usually waved my hands in front of my face while coughing loudly at my mother behind the bar. She'd roll her eyes and quickly stash the ashtray with her own cigarette beneath the bar where I wouldn't see it. The smoke would continue to swirl around her as she washed glasses and gossiped with the locals.

Nicotine had forever stained the once white curtains to a dingy shade of yellow. They hung across the windows, keeping the light of day out and the dark of night in. The fake wooden paneling on the walls added to the dreary, dismal feel of the place. I think, perhaps, it felt a bit like purgatory for the men trapped inside. Stuffed and mounted deer heads lined the walls. They were covered with a thick coat of dust and their marble-like eyeballs had lost their shine, yet they held their heads high and still looked proud and regal to a kid like me.

Every day, after school, I would do my usual walk around the bar to see what had changed overnight. I'd first stroll past the pool table, running my fingers across the cool, green felt. My eyes scoped the floor beneath the table, scanning for quarters dropped by the drunken farmers. Most days I would find one or two which I would hold up proudly for my mother to see. She would smile and give me the thumbs up and I would make my way over to the Wurlitzer jukebox in the corner.

It's flashing lights called to me like the penny slot machines at the casino enticed little old ladies to drop purse loads of coins inside. I'd pull my new found bounty out of my pants pocket and drop it into the slot. I loved the sound of the quarter plunging through the maze of mechanical springs and levers until finally dropping into the change bin at the bottom with a solid plunk.

I would spin the dial that flipped all of the song titles, reading them slowly one by one, hoping to find something new to play. I always went back to the same selections, though. A-12- *Sweet Caroline*, R-27-*Candida,*and F-17, my top personal favorite, *Sugar Sugar*, by the Archies. I would so delight in watching the 45 records spin around and around until the machine slapped the one I'd chosen onto the turntable and set the giant arm and needle onto the edge of the disc. Neil Diamond's voice would begin crooning through the fuzzy static of the worn out record, and I would continue my survey of the room, cheerfully singing along.

Every now and then, the front door would open and the bright light of day would splash into the room. Everyone seated at the bar would turn in unison, squinting into the bright light to see who had dared to intrude on their solitude. My mom would yell out a greeting from behind the bar, almost always attaching a name to the salutation. It was usually a farmer coming in off the fields—sweaty, tired, crabby, and thirsty. She knew without asking what most of these men drank and had it open and waiting before they sat down.

They would drop a stack of quarters on the bar, pinching out just enough to cover the twenty-five cent shell of beer and the seventy-five cent whiskey chaser. Everyone would look up from the bar as my mother made her way over to the ancient cash register on the back counter. She meticulously poked at the old buttons and stepped back as the drawer groaned open. The coins were graciously dropped into their slots and the drawer was closed with a muffled thud. Good service, however, did not insure a good tip. I could often hear my mother sigh as she took her place back behind the bar at the sink, washing yet another dirty glass.

The Swing

"As the moments passed, the woman on the bench wondered how this mother could be so cruel and callous."

Sitting by herself on the park bench, it seemed strange to feel so very alone while surrounded by so many people. Recently, she had begun taking daily walks through the park in an effort to shed a whopping hundred pounds — the result of twenty years of depression, alcohol, loneliness, and very poor eating habits. Having no children of her own, she often stopped at the playground to watch the toddlers run and play. The children laughed and giggled as they glided down the gleaming, silver slide.

Others closed their eyes and pumped their feet, soaring wildly through the air on the ancient park swings. The tired mothers pushed them higher and higher until it seemed like the screaming, rusty chains might snap, launching the excited youngsters off into space...of course, they did not.

She watched and wondered how her life might be now, had she not given up and shut herself off from the world. If she had not spent the best years of her life imprisoned in a body which stole from her the family she so longed for. She pondered the thought of having children of her own and quite possibly grandchildren by now. Just then, a warm summer wind brushed across her face, taking with it the single tear which fell from her eye.

Suddenly, her thoughts drifted off to childhood days and she recalled, quite vividly, her father pushing her on their backyard swing. He had looped a thick, braided rope around the broadest branch of their towering oak tree. Smiling cheerfully, he rolled an old rubber tire from behind the garage and suspended it from the dangling rope. Sitting on the grass, she watched anxiously as he thoughtfully tied and knotted the line, over and over again, making sure it would never unravel.

Finally, unable to contain herself, she blurted out, "Oh, Daddy, please can I go now? Can I just get on? " A

After pushing his large frame through the circle of the tire and taking a trial run, he awkwardly climbed out, and with great confidence, invited her aboard. Her heart pounded as his strong arms lifted her into the makeshift swing, and she thought it might leap from her chest as he shoved the tire higher and still higher into the air. She could not remember a time when she had felt so happy...so free.

As she rested on the bench, resisting the urge to get back to her two mile walk, a little girl with blonde curly hair and twinkling green eyes sat down beside her.

Wearing a pretty pink dress with an abundance of white ruffles along the bottom and shiny, white patent leather shoes, she flashed a quick smile at the woman and settled back into the seat with her short legs dangling over the edge.

They sat in silence for more than a few minutes, both staring at the children playing in the sun. The girl smiled to herself and looked longingly at the kids on the swings. Finally, when the stillness became too awkward, the woman asked, "Are you here alone? Where's your mom?"

With her eyes dancing back and forth in tempo with the swings, she pointed to a picnic table off in the distance. A woman sat there, on her phone, in exuberant conversation, ignoring the little girl as she laughed and spoke incessantly as one might do when trying to impress a potential suitor.

As the moments passed, the woman on the bench wondered how this mother could be so cruel and callous. Did she not realize the precious gift she had sitting here next to an absolute stranger on a bench in a park filled with amazing adventure? After fifteen minutes or so, the woman stood up and held out her hand to the child.

The girl looked up in silence, and in a moment of utter trust, reached out and took the woman's hand. She led her to an empty swing, lifted her into it gently, and began to push. The girl tilted her head back and giggled in delight while she relished the warm sunshine on her face. They both smiled, neither of them appreciating the fact that although they would never meet again, this single moment would become a lifelong memory for them both.

"She led her to an empty swing, lifted her into it gently, and began to push."

Postcards

"From the first glance, the first smile, the first kiss, she knew it couldn't last. In fact, she had counted on that."

They sat together on the bench, the soldier and the lady, Havanah. So much to say yet no words would suffice. It had been just three short weeks, actually nineteen days since they had met and yet it felt like an eternity. They shared splendid days in the sunshine, relaxing beside the river, strolling along the boardwalk and laughing. Her laughter made his heart pound while his smile brought a tear to her eye. Never had either felt so much tenderness or adoration for another. They relished every single moment together making them last.

He stored them away like cherished photographs to bring to mind again when had gone and the memories began to fade. They held hands and hugged and kissed until late into the evening. He wanted more, but she was a lady after all, and he respected that. He struggled for the words as they sat in silence, miserably, as their final hours together slipped by. Finally, he jumped up, grabbed her hand and pulled her to him. Holding her close, he felt her warm breath on his neck and then a single teardrop. "Will you wait for me?" he whispered in her ear. She wrapped her arms around his neck and held him close. Her mind searched for an answer...the perfect words. They would not come. She could not speak. She had so much to say, yet spoke in silent sentences.

From the first glance, the first smile, the first kiss, she knew it couldn't last. In fact, she had counted on that. She enjoyed the sudden infatuation they had both experienced when meeting that hot July evening. She had unexpectedly found herself falling for his quick wit and Kentucky charm. She had fought the feelings, as a tempestuous beehive churned inside of her stomach. Obviously there was no future with him or anyone else for that matter. She had envisioned this as just another safe, innocuous relationship.

A soldier, set to go to war; so romantically impractical. He wouldn't be looking for a commitment, or a relationship, just a good time, and that was all she could offer. That was all he would get…even if this time, with this man, she felt something more.

He pushed her away and said once again with a bit more desperation, "Will you wait for me?" His eyes narrowed as he studied her face, searching for an answer. Again she strained to find the words. Just tell him, she thought to herself. Just tell him the truth and set him free. She would not. She could not. She had never told another soul her unspeakable secret. Tonight would not be the night.

Not wanting to hurt the young man's feelings, or send him off to war with a broken heart, she held his face in her soft hands and said, "of course I will." He beamed at that and hugged her tight. They talked and planned and promised until the sun crept over the horizon. They walked hand in hand for the last time down the quiet city sidewalks toward her home. As they passed a beautiful, blooming rose bush, he reached out and plucked a perfect pink bud. He handed it to her. She flashed him a reluctant smile. Crystal teardrops fell, stretching into salty icicles of frozen apprehension. Havanah took the flower, knowing in her heart that it would be the last rose he would ever give her.

Many years later Havanah reached into the closet and pulled down a worn and tattered shoebox. Shaking hands lifted the top off the box and tenderly pulled out the pile of faded, yellow letters. There were well over a hundred, all still sealed and unopened. They were bound together with just a simple piece of twine. Havanah meticulously untied the perfect little bow, all the while staring affectionately at the one that had appeared in the mailbox just today. Havanah traced the flap along the back of the letter, tempted, yet careful not to tear it open. The crisp white envelope was placed on top of the pile and the string was delicately tied into yet another flawless bow.

The stack of letters sat there on the table for hours as the sun dropped from the sky in another unremarkable sunset. The fading daylight brought on the five o'clock shadow while he chain smoked a half a pack of Marlboros alone again in the curse of solitude. Finally, he placed them back into the tattered shoebox, being extra cautious not to crush the brittle, brown rosebud lying in the corner of the box.

To Be Normal

"I longed to experience scorching hot sand between my toes on a blistering August afternoon while I watched the searing red sun fall from the sky into Lake Huron."

As I sit here at my desk, contemplating what to share with you today. As I look out the window and watch the raindrops fall from the sky, my mind revisits a darker period of my life. It was a place where time stood still and my little office window was my only connection with the outside world. After years of massive eating rituals, I found myself weighing well over of five hundred pounds and a prisoner in my little apartment.

I spent many hours sitting in my office chair, staring at the world outside, listening to the children laugh and play below while the birds chirped and twittered above. I felt much like a goldfish confined to a tiny fishbowl, swimming in circles, day after day, while outside there were oceans, lakes, and rivers that would never be explored.

On summer days, I watched and wondered if the sunshine would ever touch my milky white skin again. Would I ever experience the marvelous sensation of the sun's intense rays warming my face and lighting up my soul? Would I walk across lush, green meadows where I might feel the cool blades of grass beneath my feet? What about the hundreds of miles of sandy beach which surround my glorious state of Michigan? I longed to experience scorching hot sand between my toes on a blistering August afternoon while I watched the searing red sun fall from the sky into Lake Huron.

As I began to shed pounds and regain my strength and stamina, I dared to dream bigger and venture even further outside of my comfort zone. I made it my purpose to enjoy, once more, the simple pleasures I had longed for. My hopes and aspirations began to change and evolve as my chains loosened. I timidly planned excursions to places I had not visited in decades—the zoo, a movie theatre, and even an art fair; simple fun for "regular" people but an exhausting adventure to someone like me.

My desires continue to change and grow as my body transforms. I wonder now, how long it will be until I am secure enough to climb aboard the pistachio green bicycle that sits in my garage, poised and ready for our maiden voyage. I dream that one day, on my daily walk through the park, my feet will find wings and push me forward fast enough to feel the thrill of running once again. I crave to feel my feet pound against the pavement while the muscles in my calves ache from fatigue…to collapse from exhaustion after having raced incessantly along the endless circle around the park.

In retrospect, I realize I am different and not like everyone else. After trying so long and so hard to fit in, I did not realize how courageous, strong, and resilient I had become. With great pride, I recognize I am a powerful human being with more resolve and steadfast determination than most "normal" people will ever possess. Today….this very moment…I say to myself, "Why settle for being normal when I have become so damn good at being extraordinary?"

Organized Chaos

"When I was at my heftiest size, it gave me eternal comfort to be able to walk into any store and ask the clerk to bring me a size 7."

For as long as I can remember, I have lived my life in a state of "organized clothing chaos." I've spent a quarter of my life in a frenzy, searching for something to wear! I continuously try on the same clothes that never... ever...manage to fit. My sizes go up...and then they go down, only to go back up once again. It's enough to drive a person mad. Looking into my walk-in closet...and then both closets in the spare bedrooms...one might think it would be easy to find SOMETHING to put on. It isn't. You see, portly people hoard clothes....it's a sickness... yes, but one that is on the rise.

I have an explanation for my disorder, as I am sure all of you will understand. First, you hang on to the outfits you once loved, even though they are old, ugly, and out of style. These are the things you pranced around in ten years ago, when you were at your smallest.

On the other end of the spectrum, you must also hold on to the absolute largest pair of pants you were ever forced to wear. You do this just in case you ever make one of those weight loss commercials posing for the camera, proud and smiling, and standing in a single pant leg. In the back of your mind, you also recall the holiday feeding frenzy you endured last winter when you gained seventeen pounds and were convinced you might be headed for those "fat" pants once again. The utter embarrassment of having to buy pants in such an enormous size causes enough anxiety to keep them folded and up on the closet shelf.

With those outfits as your anchors at each end of the size spectrum, you have everything imaginable in every conceivable size hanging there in between. "What if I go up?" you say, and better yet..."What if I go back down? What on earth will I wear if I throw everything out?" You voice this knowing a decrease in size and a big loss on the scale is indeed "just cause" for another celebratory shopping spree!! This shopping binge always includes just a "few clearance items" that aren't really your size...but will be, one day. Ahhh, and yet, another addition to your collection.

There is that one item that always seems to fit... SHOES! Big or small, like Cinderella, I can always find a pair of shoes that slide on my foot. This is why I have six totes of shoes in my basement. I literally have hundreds of pairs, many still in the box. When I was at my heftiest size, it gave me eternal comfort to be able to walk into any store and ask the clerk to bring me a size 7. This was the one, single purchase that allowed me the dignity of feeling normal and not find it necessary to whisper my size.

I suppose the saddest part of my woeful tale is the simple fact that locating something comfortable to wear from my massive collection of clothing is such an overwhelming chore, that I find myself wearing the same four shirts and my favorite pair of jeans, day after day...week after week. It is a vicious cycle indeed that I find myself immersed in. Yes....I can admit it... I am a hoarder.

Better Not Bitter

"An obscenity rushes past your lips and your cheeks turn a crimson red as the elderly woman behind the counter looks at you in horror."

There will come a day when you feel like quitting. It will quite possibly be that afternoon when you come to a group weight loss meeting, refreshed, confident, and certain you have had the most productive week one can have on the program. Reconstructing the last seven days in your mind, you tally the reasons your weigh-in will be epic. First, you skipped the neighbor's backyard barbeque on Sunday and had a salad every day for lunch. Second, you walked an extra lap around the park three times this week, and third, you followed your pre-planned menu to the letter.

You can almost hear the applause as your weight loss meeting leader hands you a star...no, TWO stars...for having such an incredible week. Oh yeah....this is about to be an epic weigh-in!

Smugly, you stroll into the office, nearly floating in those brand new pink and silver Nikes you bought last weekend; the ones that match perfectly, the trusty Fitbit strapped to your arm. Feeling like a million bucks, you stand there in line waiting for your turn. This morning, you came upon an adorable pair of jeans in the back of your closet. They slipped on quite easily today despite the fact that last month you couldn't squeeze your right butt cheek into them, even with the help of a shoehorn and a bottle of baby oil!

You smile and make small talk with the other women in line, while in your head you are searching for the perfect response to throw back at the woman behind the counter when she says, "Congratulations….that's a six pound loss this week." In your mind, you open your eyes wide and say, "Oh really!

Well, I sure wasn't expecting that," or maybe, "I guess all of my hard work *did* pay off." Finding yourself so lost in the daydream, you don't notice the annoyed cashier behind the counter and she is forced to snap her fingers in front of your face to bring you back to reality. "Step up on the scale," she barks out. Startled, you step up and gracefully mount the scale, much like Miss America accepting her crown. Finally, the woman glances up and says…nothing. NOTHING? You stare at her, waiting impatiently. "Well?" you finally blurt out.

"Well what?" she volleys back. Nervously leaning from side to side, you snarl, "Well, how much did I lose?" You feel a dab of perspiration on your forehead as you wait for her response. She looks you square in the eye and says, "You didn't. You gained a half a pound. SEE?" and she slides your weekly tracker under your nose. You glance down and see it, right there in black and white. An obscenity rushes past your lips and your cheeks turn a crimson red as the elderly woman behind the counter looks at you in horror. The room has gone silent and you become quite uncomfortable as everyone turns to stare. So many emotions come over you, and what's worse, you feel as though you just gained forty pounds, instead of just half of one. You scramble off of the scale and slink to the back of the room where you hang your head and tiptoe out the door, skipping the meeting entirely.

Everyone has found themselves there, on that scale, expecting a huge loss but gaining instead. We have all felt so defeated that we went home without even staying for our weekly words of wisdom. It happens. Deal with it, accept it, and change it. This is not the time to quit or take a break from the program. These are the days when you look beyond the number and see the value in your other accomplishments.

For instance, appreciate the reality that you were able to fit into those adorable jeans today. Maybe you should think about the extra laps you were capable of walking around the park this week, when just six short months ago you thought you might have a coronary while walking across the Walmart parking lot.

Focus on the positive and work a little harder this week, and if that doesn't work, force yourself to remember how you felt walking through those front doors and stepping up on that dark and ominous scale for the VERY FIRST TIME. Stop, take a breath, and tell yourself, "I must never....ever...go back to that."

The Zoo

"Humiliated and embarrassed, you suck your stomach in and reach your hands above your head, hoping to squeeze yourself through the stupid spinning gate...it is that very moment that you begin to question your sanity and your absurd decision to visit the zoo."

I decided to stray a bit from my daily walk in the park and turn my hike into an adventure. It had been a long time since I considered a trip to the Detroit Zoo...decades, actually. Walking the trails through the animal reserve when you weigh more than five hundred pounds is not an excursion one looks forward to, but instead cunningly avoids. An ancient rerun of Wild Kingdom or visit to the Animal Planet channel was enough of a safari for me back in my rounder, five hundred pounder days.

There were numerous difficulties associated with such a trip. First of all, imagine, if you will, picking up a full grown St. Bernard, strapping him to your back, and then for fun...picking up another one and throwing him over your shoulder. This should put you close to my enormous breadth. Now, take a walk around the block and see if that doesn't put you into cardiac arrest. If not, great...you are on your way to a fun-filled day! Next, load you (and your St. Bernards) into a vehicle, drive out to your destination, and prepare to park a half mile from the gate...if you're lucky.

Get out, tighten up your sneakers, and head for the ticket booth. Be sure to wear sunblock, as this trek may take a good forty-five minutes, since most of your traveling is done in "low" gear.

Eventually, you will reach the ticket window, sweating profusely and panting where you will be greeted by Tiffany, an obnoxiously happy, one hundred ten pound, perfectly beautiful young lady. She will smile gleefully and ask if you are okay and you will bitterly throw your money at her and wheeze away from the window.

As you pass through the gate, feeling as though you have already run a 5K, you are tempted to make a U-turn and go right back until you find yourself stuck in the little turnstile that everyone else seems to glide through. Humiliated and embarrassed, you suck your stomach in and reach your hands above your head, hoping to squeeze yourself through the stupid spinning gate…it is that very moment that you begin to question your sanity and your absurd decision to visit the zoo.

This was a chapter from the story of my life before joining Weight Watchers a few years back. Years later, and two hundred fifty pounds lighter, I am looking forward to my first visit to the Detroit Zoo in nearly two decades. My daily walks have prepared me for this little field trip, and I feel enthusiastic and eager to begin this exploration. I arm myself with just a Nikon camera and a pedometer. I choose to go on a quiet Tuesday afternoon, when I know the place won't be overrun with evil, screaming children.

The sun feels warm while the air is cool and it is a perfect day for such an adventure. As I pass through the entrance, I hand my money to the woman at the window and deviously smile to myself when I realize she is both older and chubbier than me. I am also pleased to find that the turnstiles have been removed, though I am quite sure I would have slid through with ease.

Strolling along, I take my time…not because I am weary, exhausted, or because I may stroke out from the heat. In all honesty, I am thoroughly enjoying my time spent with the lions, camels, and the zebras who are taking afternoon naps in the sun. Taking a cue from the animals, I stop to sit and rest on the solid wooden benches carved out of pine and cedar.

Relaxing peacefully, I listen to the birds sing, surrounded by the scent of a thousand exquisite wildflowers, plants, and sweet-smelling blossoms and I spot a sleepy gorilla lying on a rock. I laugh to myself as I realize he reminds me of "yours truly" not so very long ago.

Finally, it is late in the day and the sun has become a red wafer in the sky. In the distance, I hear the whistle blow on the little train which circles the park. I remember on my last visit, I had been afraid to try and board the train for fear of falling, or even worse, not fitting into the seat. Today, on this day, I wait for the locomotive to stop, and I confidentially stroll up to the boarding gate and step up onto the train.

I slide back into the seat quite comfortably, and smile as I listen to the wheels churn and feel the cool wind hit my face.

Appreciate the Little Things

"Loyalty is more than just a word...it is an instinct you are born with. You can't be a "little" loyal any more than you can be a "little" sorry."

Today, I find myself at the close of another year, facing a new beginning. Appreciate the little things...marvel at the big. Realize that your heart grows along with age, making room for tolerance, mercy, and compassion. Take a look back at your life and learn to forgive the people you love for the mistakes they have made. Don't forget to include yourself, as you see that you have made quite a few as well.

Loyalty is more than just a word...it is an instinct you are born with. You can't be a "little" loyal any more than you can be a "little" sorry. Either you are or you aren't. Honor your real friends. You will find that although you have over two thousand Facebook friends, you can count your real friends on one hand—two if you're lucky. As time slips past, there will be lovers and lost loves. You will sometimes think about the ones you thought you loved and shed a tear over the one you "know" you loved...and then lost. You will sit and ponder over what lies ahead, while believing the best has past. Today is a day of reflection...tomorrow will be a time of change.

There will be turning points as you embrace the excitement of a new journey on the horizon. Ignore the anxious feeling inside, even if it makes your heart pound and your mind race. Dare to dream. Take the chance to explore the unknown and see the unseen.

No one ever knows what's up ahead, but you have already lived the life behind you. There's no turning back. The joy and the wonders of life are always just out of reach. Never stop searching, or learning, or loving. Learn to appreciate the moments of your life for you will never, ever have enough.

The Hourglass

"You squander time as though it were
boundless…limitless…endless."

I found myself experiencing a bit of melancholy this evening. Too much time spent recalling misplaced friends and days gone by left me feeling rather hollow and empty. When you are young, you think you have all the time in the world to achieve your dreams and reach your goals.

You squander time as though it were boundless...limitless...endless.

Projects initiated so enthusiastically lie abandoned midway through. You give up all too easily on lovers and friendships when things become awkward or difficult. Of course, you call it a "break". Endings are just too harsh for the young. A break seems much less messy and unpleasant.

The truth is, it's just a way of letting go without admitting that you are giving up. You hold that little piece of "I'll get back to it" in the back of your mind...or "we just need a little space." Don't believe it. More often than not, it's simply a crutch. You can't go back because the rest of the world has already moved forward. Circumstances change. People change. It seems to make the break less painful when you leave yourself or others with that tiny speck of promise.

Hope, after all, is the key to life. Sometimes, hope is the bridge you use to cross over to that next person, that next job...or that next city. It gives you a false sense of security. Believing you can turn back actually pushes one forward. It is much easier to walk across a tight wire when there is a net stretched out beneath you or jump through the clouds with a parachute on your back.

When I was young, I was fearless. Time was like money in the bank. With my time I bought experience. I bought knowledge. I learned how to meld the two into power. That power gave me the strength to find myself, and in turn, live my truth. For that opportunity, I am grateful. There will be poignant days, like today, in which nostalgia will move me to the verge of tears. I do not cry for what I have left behind in my life, but instead for all that I shall never discover.

While time may be infinite for the universe as a whole, we are given but an hourglass filled with a measured amount of sand. Even as I write this in my journal, my sand is sliding through the timepiece. There is no way to slow it down. There is no way to stop it. Perhaps I would be wise to take my shoes off and just slide my toes into the sand and simply enjoy the moment. Maybe I should....but I just don't have the time

The Edge

And with a breathless promise, your seduction lured me in.
You stole my soul, and trapped it whole,
There inside my virgin skin.
Glassy eyed, I stepped outside and stood on twilight's ledge.
A one night stand, you grabbed my hand,

As I inched closer to the edge.
I lingered in the darkness, afraid that I might fall,
Hypnotized and tranquilized,
My back against the wall.

And still you had this hold on me, so able to entice,
The treasured sin that pulled me in
It came at quite a price.
All that I had worked for began to slip away,

The reality, of my mortality,
Did so consume my days.
I look now to my future, there's nothing there to see,
I've sat and cried, thinking suicide
Was all that's left for me.

Oh yes, you kept your promise, you said you'd never leave,
And when I'm gone, you'll linger on.
You'll be right there to grieve.

A Misplaced Memory

"You cannot predict a memory. You never realize when one is in the making until it is too late to change it. The randomness of the recollection is what makes it so profound."

Today I thought about my mother. It was easier than it was at this time last year. I am coming upon the third anniversary of her passing. I remember because it was May 5, 2012, Cinco de Mayo, a day of celebration for much of the world, the worst day of my life for me.

You cannot predict a memory. You never realize when one is in the making until it is too late to change it. The randomness of the recollection is what makes it so profound. What renders an event something you will retain as a memory for the rest of your life? Your world evolves and changes incessantly. Every single moment is singular, distinctive, and unique. Every sight, sound, smell, and emotion becomes a part of that particular memory. It all fits together like a filmstrip or an old and faded photo album sitting on a bookshelf. Often it lies there for years—even decades—lingering, waiting, and dwelling there in a patient state of perpetual readiness, anticipating that opportune moment when it is most necessary or convenient for one to retrieve it.

The happiest times I shared with my mother, be that during the winter holidays or in her living room watching silly comedies as we laughed so hard tears fell from our eyes, came back. Those were followed by those poignant memories of my sister and me sitting beside her, grief-stricken, as she wasted away in a hospital bed. For a time, I could not separate the two. The good brought on the bad as though they were linked together as intensely as thunder and lightning, or as stubbornly as peanut butter and jelly.

Try as I might, I could not enjoy the good without the bad creeping in and taking over, so I shut them both out. Sadly, I stopped thinking about my mother. Making a concentrated effort, I avoided photographs and steadfastly walked past the office cupboard, which was filled with snapshots and Polaroids, sentimental birthday cards and encouraging letters she had sent to me in college. Somehow, I "accidentally" misplaced the silver framed photo that had sat on my desk for several years before she passed—the same picture I had glanced at literally thousands of times while I toiled away at my computer making deals and writing papers.

And then one day, while clearing a spot on my desk, I came upon the framed photo of her that I had somehow managed to bury under a mound of paper, and the memories came flooding back. They began to bounce and ricochet inside of my head faster than I could comprehend or begin to grasp. There was no time to sort or organize, catalogue or classify. I collapsed into my caramel colored office chair and stared at the surreptitious photograph.

My hand shook just the tiniest bit as I reached over and tugged open the little cupboard above my desk. My mother's own personal photo album fell into my lap. I had not had the heart nor the courage to open this album after she had passed, and now here it was, in my hands, imploring me to do just that. Feeling quite vulnerable, I ran my fingers across the faded cover, deliberating my choice to open the old book or just put it back.

Opening it, I saw my mother's smiling face holding my brother when he was but a baby. As I turned the page, I spotted a photo of her at the kitchen table, laughing so hard her eyes were just slits perched on top of her bright red cheeks, and then, without warning, I saw the snapshot of us, together, smiling at the camera with our arms interlocked. It was then I realized that seeing those pictures made me smile. They forced the last memories I had of my mother in that hideous hospital gown to the deepest, darkest part of my brain while pushing these happier times to the front of my consciousness.

I began to understand that I needed to see these photos and share her memories. Woefully, I recognized that hiding her away was only hurting me. Abruptly, I reached over and dusted off the silver photo frame which surrounded my favorite picture of her and put it right next to me on my desk, where I would see her every day and secretly thank her for giving me the inner strength to do so.

Gone Too Soon

"One day, your life will inevitably flash before your eyes. Like a filmstrip running through your mind, you will watch yourself grow up and then grow old."

In every life, there comes a time when we reach the unfortunate realization that the days that lay behind us far outnumber those we have before us. It slaps you, much like a cold blast of January wind might as you step outside on a frosty winter morning. It is this very day you begin to take stock of your life. Your mind struggles to recall all the places you have seen, the people you have loved, and the things you have done. While your mind revisits the past, your heart considers the future, and like it or not, it begins to compile a list of its own, the infamous "bucket list." It is an irrational, interminable list, for as your years grow shorter, the list grows eternally longer, until one day you realize you will never have enough time to accomplish all you have squared and tallied.

One day, your life will inevitably flash before your eyes. Like a filmstrip running through your mind, you will watch yourself grow up and then grow old. You will remember the thundering magnificence of Niagara Falls and the reverence of the Great Smokey Mountains at daybreak and recollect the feeling of the warm white sand beneath your feet and the cool chill of the ocean waves that licked at your ankles as the tide rolled in. In silent serenity, you will again see the countless sunsets which colored the evening sky with brilliant layers of orange, red and yellow; you will be at peace.

Looking back, you will not remember the conference call you had last night, or the pizza you devoured for dinner, and you will have absolutely no recollection of the incalculable hours you spent in front of the television set just wishing you had the energy to take your pleading little dog for a walk. Regretfully, you'll lose track of the countless morning sunrises squandered as you lay in bed until noon, sleeping off another hangover.

Life is short and time is precious. We are granted but a basket full of priceless days to experience the miraculous and extraordinary gifts we have been given. The beauty of this world is astounding and perpetual. You could live the rest of your life waking to an exquisite sunrise in a different city, state, or country every single morning and yet, not begin to comprehend all you will miss.

It is not too late to turn your life around. Start today…right now and make the necessary changes for you to begin living again. In your heart, you know what you are doing to yourself—these bad habits you nurture—are stealing your life…your days…your hours. Make a plan, say a prayer, take a step, and turn your life around.

When they place the headstone on your grave, don't let the eulogist declare, "Poor old gal, she's gone too soon. There's not much else to say." Instead, let your friends and family exclaim with elation to the world, "Rest in peace, my fearless friend…it's hard to say goodbye. You lived and laughed, but most of all…you sure knew how to fly!"

Just Listen

"As I pondered my future, or lack of one, I would listen to the ticking of my kitchen clock, and when the silence became too deafening to bear..."

There was a time when I weighed well over five hundred pounds. Fearing ridicule, I began to venture out less and less. There came a day when leaving the apartment was no longer an option. I sat alone in silence most days, wondering what my purpose might be, because, after all, everyone has a purpose, don't they?

As I pondered my future, or lack of one, I would listen to the ticking of my kitchen clock, and when the silence became too deafening to bear, I would struggle across the room and slide open my patio door to invite the outer world inside for a visit. I would listen to the chorus of birds singing outside my window and I would smile and listen to the children below, laughing in delight on a warm summer afternoon. How I longed to feel the sunshine on my face.

Today, much smaller and much healthier, resting on a park bench, I write quietly in my worn and weathered journal. I sit and listen to the water from the river rush past while the ducks and geese harmonize above. In the distance, I hear the frantic clanging of a railroad crossing as the train rolls past, offering up a lonely bellow. As I rise to continue my daily stroll, I hear the leaves crunching beneath my feet and realize that fall is just around the corner. Stopping for an instant, I take a deep breath, and am thankful for this single moment of peaceful freedom. Then, tilting my face up to the sky, I smile as the sun warms my cheeks and I listen intently to the world, the earth, and my heart whisper..."Welcome back...where have you been?"

Camping

"To go camping when you are three times the size of the average human being is a calamity of misfortune just waiting to happen. Climbing up the rickety little steps and squeezing through the hobbit-sized door of a camper is only the beginning."

There I was, sitting next to a blazing campfire still feeling a slight chill as the July sun fell from the sky. It left behind splashes and streaks of crimson and ginger to welcome the midsummer moon as it ascended into the heavens. A marshmallow turned black and crispy on the crooked stick I held above the flames as I sat there and relished the smell of the burning timber and the syrupy scent of pinecones while the sound of the river murmured in the distance. Content, I sat in the company of old friends as we smiled and laughed and spoke of days gone by. There was a delightful sense of peace and tranquility which surrounded my heart and enveloped my soul.

And then the sudden crash of thunder forced me from my dream and dropped me back into reality. Opening my eyes, I found myself looking past my feet to the babbling show which filled the television screen in front of me. Sadly, I realized all too soon that I was once again sitting in my living room, imprisoned in my old brown recliner, empty and alone. Squeezing my eyes closed, I tried frantically to recapture the simple freedom of my dream and could not.

To go camping when you are three times the size of the average human being is a calamity of misfortune just waiting to happen. Climbing up the rickety little steps and squeezing through the hobbit-sized door of a camper is only the beginning. Cramming yourself into the closet-sized bathroom and trying to shower when your massive body fills the tiny stall is a whole new chapter of this dismal story. Sitting around the campfire in one of the standard little white plastic chairs will turn into a fiasco when it collapses from the sudden impact of four hundred pounds squeezing into it.

The walking, the swimming, even climbing into the rowboat sitting at the dock is a comical catastrophe in the making. You realize that camping will just be one too many "UH-OH" moments strung together. You sigh as you heave yourself out of the chair and lumber off to bed, realizing the only fire you will enjoy tonight is the little pine scented candle on the nightstand.

Etheltrude Isabella

"The old steps groaned and squeaked as we made our way to the top. I reached for the old brass doorknob and gave it a twist. The door creaked open a bit, and then I let go of the handle. The door swung wide and what I saw made me feel a bit dizzy."

Etheltrude Isabella—what kind of a name was that, anyway? Who would torture their kid with a name like that? For hours, I tried to imagine just what a woman with such a horrid name would look like and still, I had no idea of who or what to expect. All I had were the childhood memories my mother had shared with us through the years—the tales about her bossy older sister whose side of the bedroom was always a mess.

Bored and restless, I kicked the seat in front of me, knowing full well it would result in an evil look and an angry warning from my mother. I didn't care, though...I was irritated. Why wouldn't she be? I had been forced to endure seven long hours sitting in the back seat of our Chevy Impala, stuck to the thick, plastic seat cover. Seven dreary hours filled with bouts of car sickness, hunger, thirst, and my nagging little sister beside me. I could feel my backside developing a heat rash from the friction of the hot and sticky seat covers. Extreme discomfort combined with asphyxiation—thanks to my father's chain smoking—made this fun family getaway less than tolerable. Sitting there, annoyed, in the blanket of cigarette smoke, kicking and coughing, I wondered how much longer I could conceivably endure this much family fun.

"How much longer until we get there?" I bellowed from the back seat.

"Almost there," answered my mother in a less than convincing voice.

"Mom! You've been saying that all day! For real, now, how much longer?" I whined.

Noticing my father's shoulders tense up as he maneuvered our car through endless rows of station wagons and semi-trucks, I looked up and caught a shot of his steel gray eyes glaring at me in the rearview mirror. Nervously, I sat back and crossed my arms, knowing what would happen if Dad felt the need to insert his opinion. Cringing, I waited for his harsh words. Instead, he reached for one of the open packs of Viceroy Cigarettes on the dashboard and turned up the Johnny Cash tune on the radio. Gratefully, I breathed a small sigh of relief and squeezed my eyes shut in an attempt to fall asleep. My little sister, half awake and sucking her thumb, laid her head on my arm and quickly fell asleep. We'd get there when we got there, and that's all there was to that.

Unsure of how much time had passed, I was awakened by the sound of loud voices and adult laughter. Opening first one eye and then the other, I peered out of the car window and could see a whole lot of hugging, hand shaking, and back slapping going on. Apparently, we had finally arrived in Kenosha. Suddenly, my mom popped open the door on my side of the car, smiling. "Alana, Diana...wake up...wake up! I want you to meet my sister, your Aunt Ethel!"

She reached in and pulled me across the backseat and out the car door. Still groggy, I turned around just in time to find my face buried in the gigantic torso of a woman who most certainly must be the mysterious Aunt Etheltrude (Aunt Ethel, for short). I felt her massive arms encircle me and I immediately felt suffocated by a peculiar scent of lilac perfume mixed with cabbage and onions. I had not yet seen her face, but I could see she was dressed in a wrinkled, yellow and white paisley shirt and very tight yellow stretch pants. I squirmed and thrashed for my freedom while she relentlessly mashed my face into her Jell-O like form.

I broke loose and abruptly stepped back behind my little sister, pushing her forward in a sacrificial offering to this hulking figure with outstretched arms. I narrowed my eyes and felt my forehead wrinkle as I saw, for the first time, the mysterious relative I had heard about my entire life. To my surprise, she was nothing I had expected.

Ethel was my mother's only sister. She was in her late 40's and must have weighed over four hundred pounds. She had developed a pigeon-toed stance to help balance her hulking figure. Her hair was permed tightly, which in turn made her head look tiny perched upon that huge body. Her breathing was heavy and labored and sometimes she could not seem to catch her breath. This was especially noticeable when she had one of her laughing attacks and she had many.

Everyone loved to make her laugh. It was contagious and even though she coughed, wheezed, and sputtered, everyone pushed the joke just a little bit further to enjoy the frenzied sensation of one of Ethel's uncontrollable bouts of hysteria. She would go on and on and finally stop to catch her breath. With tears rolling down her cheeks, she'd gasp, "Oh, for the love of God!" At that point, we knew the attack had run its course and we could all settle back down into pleasant conversation.

My Uncle Pete was the center of Aunt Ethel's universe. Pete was an enormous man who seldom spoke but always smiled and towered over everyone, including Ethel. My uncle had spent most of his adult life working in the Kenosha Steel Mill and would undoubtedly stay there until he retired or his back gave out. They had a homely daughter, my cousin, Mary Ann, who ironically ran a beauty shop in town. She was thirty and still lived with her mom and dad and a chubby little black and white Chihuahua named Tiny.

Happy to be released from my prison, and eager to relieve myself, I ran toward the house.

"Alana...no...no...no, honey, come back! You can't go in there right now."

I skidded to a halt and turned back to see if she were kidding. She wasn't.

"But, Mom, I have to use the bathroom!" I screamed.

My mother came after me and grabbed my hand and yanked me toward the Impala.

"Aunt Ethel has a nice little room for us down the street at the Motel 6," she mumbled to me as she pushed me back into the car. My father drove down to the little motel, which is where we stayed for the next two days.

Aunt Ethel, Uncle Pete, and Mary Ann rotated in and out of the motel over the next couple days. They took us places around town, like the park and the Piggly Wiggly, but I wondered why we were spending all our time visiting in a cramped motel room when they had a huge two story house we could explore and enjoy. I asked my mom, but she did not have an answer, either.

Finally, the time came to pack up and head back to Michigan. We loaded up the car and my mother insisted on taking one last swing by Pete and Ethel's to say goodbye. It would probably be a very long time before we saw them again. And in fact, it was. It was nine long years.

We rolled into the gravel driveway and they came out onto the porch to greet us, pulling the door shut behind them. Uncle Pete arranged the lawn chairs in the front yard under the big oak tree and the adults sat together to reminisces and speak of old times.

Bored with the conversation, Diana and I wandered off to explore the back yard. After a time, I realized I had to use the bathroom. I thought about what had happened the last time I had asked and decided that I would just go in and use it on my own. I grabbed my sister's hand and pulled her along with me as I made my way up the steps to the back door. It felt like we were doing something wrong. The huge white door loomed in front of us. I stopped for just a minute and then started up.

The old steps groaned and squeaked as we made our way to the top. I reached for the old brass doorknob and gave it a twist. The door creaked open a bit, and then I let go of the handle. The door swung wide and what I saw made me feel a bit dizzy. Behind me, I heard Diana gasp and felt her grip my hand tighter as we peered into the darkened room mesmerized by what we saw.

After a long minute of utter silence, we stepped inside. I thought that perhaps the shadows of the early evening were playing tricks on my eyes. Soon after they had adjusted to the darkened room, I realized they were not.

The space was filled...from the floor to the ceiling...with brown paper shopping bags. There were bags on top of bags on top of faded brown boxes. Bags full of clothes and dishes and puzzles and shoes. There were hundreds and hundreds of balls of brightly colored yarn packed into brown paper Piggly Wiggly grocery bags. The smell of the room was suffocating. I could feel my heart pounding inside of my chest. I glanced around the room, dumbfounded. My mind told me to turn and run. It implored me to flee this house and never look back; however, my feet stood firm as if surrounded by quicksand.

I scanned to my left. The entire wall was filled with shelves. They were stocked with glass candy jars of all shapes and sizes. Most were clear, displaying the candy inside. Jars upon jars filled with silver wrapped candy Kisses, gumballs, Tootsie Rolls, Dum Dums, squares of Bazooka bubble gum, and so much more. I had never in my life seen anything like it.

The tables and chairs were covered with magazines and newspapers, junk mail and books. There was a path cutting through the walls of bags and boxes...wide enough to get to the next room.

Diana wrapped her arms around my waist, sobbing slightly and held even tighter as I followed the path through the house. We were surrounded by "stuff" that reached to the ceiling. Every door we opened led to another room filled to capacity, even the stairway was so jammed with bags and clothes and books that we did not dare attempt to climb them. My little sister became overwhelmed and ran from the house crying. I chased her, happy to get out of the nightmare myself, slamming the door behind us.

Many years had passed before I told anyone about Aunt Ethel's house. And when I did, I don't think anyone really believed me. I had many bad dreams and nightmares as a kid about that house, mostly about being trapped inside. We never made our way back to Kenosha.

As I grew older and thought about the house and the family inside, it made me sad. Aunt Ethel was actually a warm and wonderful woman who would do anything for her family. She sent us cards and letters along with a crisp five dollar bill inside of a colorful birthday card every year after that. She came to visit a few times, too.

As the years went on and the memory of her overflowing home faded, I grew to love Aunt Ethel. I sadly realized that my dear aunt had spent her entire life a prisoner, trapped inside a body that suffocated her soul and a house which imprisoned her spirit.

The Pistachio Green Bicycle

"I could see people in the aisles trying not to stare, but they watched inquisitively from the corner of their eyes. As I studied the pistachio green stallion, I suddenly realized we were meant for one another"

Walking aimlessly through the aisles of the local department store, I turn the corner and come upon a flourish of shiny metallic bicycles all uniformly lined and double stacked in magnificent rows of splendor. The smell of rubber overcomes me and I am immersed back in time to a long forgotten childhood memory.

Instantly, I visualize myself racing along the sidewalks of my beloved hometown on my little orange Huffy with black racing stripes, high handlebars, and a long black banana seat. Listening to the tires whirling beneath me as my feet frantically pump the rubber pedals, I can feel the wind rush against my face when suddenly… "PRICE-CHECK-HOMEGOODS," crackles brashly across the intercom speakers overhead and I come crashing down, back into the toy department.

Staring wistfully at the glorious procession of shiny red racers and elegant black mountain bikes, my heart pounds and then, I spot it….a rather unattractive, pistachio green Huffy Cruiser. With no fancy gear shifts or shiny chrome accessories, along with that hideous pistachio color, it did not fit in. I studied its big, sturdy tires and the enormous white seat which rested snugly atop a layer of curly springs. It had character, that was for sure. It stood there alone, among the sleek specimens of modern technology, proud, strong, and sturdy, much like myself.

It seemed like a hundred years since the thought of riding a bicycle had even crossed my mind, yet something drew me to it. I reached out and touched the soft leather seat and then I clutched the white rubber handlebar grips.

They felt glorious in my hands as I slowly rolled the contraption from its designated place in line, much like one would lead a thoroughbred out of its stable. As I gently popped the kickstand down, I could see people in the aisles trying not to stare, but they watched inquisitively from the corner of their eyes. As I studied the pistachio green stallion, I suddenly realized we were meant for one another.

I knew in my heart I might never have the courage to actually climb upon that majestic cruiser to take a ride, and yet I rolled it proudly through the store and to the front register. As I handed the cashier my money, I thought to myself, "Sometimes, starting one's life over means doing things for the first time....again."

Letting Go

"There came a day when I felt I might suffocate myself with Charlie. I could see my life slipping away. I looked at him with loathing as we sat in silence and stuffed ourselves to the point of intoxication."

Well, the divorce is final! Let me explain. I spent twenty-five years in an oppressive, controlling, stifling, and very demoralizing relationship with "my other half". By other half, I mean that two hundred fifty pounds of extra body weight that all but smothered me. It somehow took on a life of its own and eventually took away mine in the process. Let's call that other half Charlie.

Charlie was a gleeful soul at first. We spent lots of time together and had fun eating and drinking to our hearts' content, loosening our belts as they became tighter and tighter. Charlie's philosophy was always "Go big or go home" and boy oh boy did we ever live by that principle. We did everything to the extreme—extra-large pizzas smothered in extra cheese, double quarter pounders with cheese...super-sized, please.

As time went on, we began spending all of our time together. Charlie became so possessive. It got to the point where he would not let me leave the house. I could not see my friends or visit with my family. We stayed home all the time. We did not go on dates—no movies, carnivals, or concerts. "We have a big screen TV," he said..."What else do we need?" Like the devil, he seduced me in to staying home and accommodating his needs....oh, and he was oh so needy!

I became mournful and miserable. My life had no meaning or purpose. My purpose had become feeding Charlie...my captor. Don't get me wrong, he gave me things, too...anxiety, paranoia, high blood pressure, depression, and in return I gave him my health, my happiness, and my freedom. There came a day when I felt I might suffocate myself with Charlie. I could see my life slipping away. I looked at him with loathing as we sat in silence and stuffed ourselves to the point of intoxication. We were indeed a TOXIC couple. One night, I asked him for a trial separation. Oh, he fought like the dickens to hold on to me, playing head games and mental manipulation. I fought back. I joined Weight Watchers, began walking, and went back to school and slowly began taking my life back.

Charlie continued to hang around ...to hold on, tempt, and entice. As I became stronger and healthier, I began to see less and less of him. So today, I declare my independence! My divorce is final! Charlie, my "other half" who, by the way, is most certainly not my "better" half, is officially gone and out of my life. He won't be back. Goodbye and good riddance. I realize today, that I only held on because I was afraid to let go.

The Good Stuff

"Life is about the "Choice" not the "Reward"

There will be days when you will want to give up. Walking away will seem much easier than hanging on. You will tire of the day to day struggle you endure to keep moving forward and inevitably wonder to yourself, "Why is it so hard to just be normal?" It will be on this dark and dreary day that you will close your eyes to who you are, and instead, beat yourself up for who you are not.

You may have forgotten the pain your body endured every morning as you hauled your massive body out of bed. Remember how your knees and ankles crackled and popped when you stepped down on the bedroom floor? Do you recall when your current "Fat" pants were so tight you could not even get the zipper up? How about family shopping sprees at the mall? While everyone zipped in and out of store after store, you picked from the three hideous outfits they carried in your size at the "Mundane Bryant" store for portly women. Remember how the steering wheel of your car rubbed your stomach every time you turned a corner and how a flight of stairs turned your legs to jelly? Yep, that was your life. Sometimes we forget.

No, every day is not a perfect day. Weeks may come and go when you are stalled and nothing has happened. You must keep in mind, that every time you step on the scale, there is no promise it will go down or a guarantee that just because you showed up for your Weight Watchers meeting, it will never go up.

Whether you are losing or gaining, life goes on, and as long as you are alive and breathing, there will be temptation. There will be graduation parties, Thanksgiving feasts, and let's not forget, grandma's delectable Christmas cookies. Your little ghosts and goblins will return home with bags of bite-size candy bars and yummy popcorn balls every Halloween night, and when your birthday rolls around this year, will you honestly be able to say no to a little slice of your favorite butter cream frosted birthday cake? It is safe to say...probably not. Food is a huge component of celebration and camaraderie, and let's face it, the center of all of our holiday traditions. Is it really fair to have to give it all up? The good stuff... isn't that what life is all about?

You obviously cannot boycott the family Thanksgiving dinner or strawberry shortcake for the rest of your life; however, you can learn to focus on the *quality* of what you choose instead of the *quantity*. A bite of everything on the Thanksgiving table will have to satisfy what the eleven pound plate of stuffing, mashed potatoes, and gravy once did. You cannot succeed on this lifetime journey of salvation and self-preservation without rewarding yourself every now and again.

One of the greatest lessons you can learn is to savor that first bite. Your taste buds were created to focus on the first sweet or salty taste of everything you eat. They dance in elation when you let the first bit of food linger on your tongue; nothing is quite as tasty after that. So why not make your life all about the first morsel...the first nibble….the first bite? When your sweetheart gives you that heart-shaped box of chocolates on Valentine's Day, look for your favorite piece.

Consider and contemplate, relish the aroma, and then carefully choose. Savor the choice and enjoy that single piece of heavenly chocolate. You will eventually learn life is all about the choice and not the reward, and you will be so much happier when you learn to appreciate the experience instead of the indulgence.

Big Top Blues

I've traveled these roads for forty-three years,
From village, to city, to town,
It seems that all we ever do
Is build up, and then just as quickly, tear down
We silently roll in together,
In the darkness of the night,
The campers, the trailers,
Vendors and entertainers
The big tent rolled up, nice and tight
And while you lay in bed sleeping,
Dreaming so content,
The signs go up
The stakes go down,
And the circus becomes an event.
The children wake up in the morning,
Wipe their eyes and stretch with a yawn,
Enticed by the scent of warm cotton candy
They put on their shoes and are gone!
As for me, I sit in my trailer,
Eating breakfast all alone.
I have no wife or family life
Just this empty tin can I call home.
I remember when I was a young boy,
Watching from the stands,
The tumblers the jugglers and acrobats,
All under the ringmasters command.
When suddenly he came out of nowhere,

And filled up that big center ring,
With colorful clothes,
And a squeaky red nose,
He did a cartwheel and a handspring!
A thunderous applause rose around me,
The crowd jumped to their feet and went wild,
That clown did inspire, in my heart, a desire
As I stood there in awe, just a child,
So here I stand, decades later,
A lonely and crumbling old man,
My life's a charade, one big masquerade
This sure wasn't part of the plan.
Bad mood, bad day?
It doesn't matter

The audience doesn't care,
They've paid good money to laugh at me,
That's the reason that they are there.
I sit here in the mirror,
And a tear falls from my eye,
I wipe it away, no not today,
The kids can't see me cry.
I paint a smile upon my face,
To cover up my frown,
The happiest place on earth? Maybe,
But not for this lonely old clown.

Albert O'Malley

"Albert knew in his heart, though, that in reality he would probably spend the next couple days nursing his weathered body back to health, and she would be there beside him, rubbing his back and bringing him hot tea with honey."

Albert O'Malley carefully slid the old fishing boat alongside the dilapidated dock. The seagulls screamed overhead while the salty sea air filled his lungs. He skillfully tossed the knotted rope around the post and pulled the boat in tight. It felt good to be home after three days on the water. This trip had been unusually exhausting, causing him to wonder if it might be his last. However, Albert knew this was typical and after a couple days on land his heart would once again crave the absolute freedom of the sea, or would it?

He stood on deck, trying to straighten his aching back. He had developed a stoop while out on the boat. The constant heaving and rolling of the vessel forced him to lean forward in an effort to keep his balance. After three days of fighting the wind and waves, he'd find himself bent over at the waist, unable to stand up. Albert's hands and feet were swollen. His fingers raw and bleeding from the ropes he spent his days pulling out of the ocean were further tortured by the salt water that seeped into every cut and crevasse.

He pulled his aching body to the edge of the boat and struggled over the side onto the sagging wharf. It had become a difficult task over the last couple years. His bones ached all of the time now—so much that his dear wife, Catherine, had started begging him to pass the lobster boat on to their boys, Shane and Ennis.

"Dahlin'," she would say in her thick "Cape Codders" accent, "Ya don't hafta wook so haad anymore! Da boys know how to catch dem old lobstahs. It's time for you ta spend some time hea, at home, wit me." She would lovingly hold his hard and calloused hands inside of hers. The years had carved many lines into her face and turned her beautiful red locks to a silver gray. Her eyes, however, were still as blue as the first time he had looked into them and her smile was as beautiful as ever. He knew she was the best thing that had ever happened to him. He just found it so hard to show her.

"Awwww, mind ya own business, woman," he would growl at her. "I got ten good yeas left in me, so quit ya nagging." He'd stand up and march out the door and straight down to Kelly's Pub where he'd sit drinking and swapping fishing stories with the locals until long after Catherine had gone to sleep. Eventually, Albert would stagger home and slip in the back door, stoke the fire a bit, tossing on another log, and fall asleep in his favorite chair, never realizing that his dear Catherine had once again cried herself to sleep.

Albert had met Catherine just about thirty-seven years ago. They were both in their late twenties when they bumped into each other, quite by accident, in the Mercantile. She had been reaching for a jar of peaches on the top shelf. Albert, not paying attention, backed into her, while counting the money he had just been paid by the shopkeeper for a basket of fresh Cod.

The jar of peaches crashed to the floor, along with Catherine. "Watch whea ya going, mista!" she had shouted at him. Startled, he swiftly bent over to help her up. He reached out and grabbed her delicate hand. She looked up from the mess that surrounded her and their eyes locked together. She felt herself gasp and then stared in silence. For Albert, everything stopped right there at that moment and he knew that he had found the woman he would spend the rest of his life with.

Catherine loved Albert with all of her heart. She would not have chosen to spend the last thirty-some years with anyone else. However, their life had been far from perfect. For her, it was a reclusive, lonely life spent waiting. Waiting for Albert to leave, waiting for him to come home. Waiting for him to wake up and waiting for him to finish eating. He was gone most days and home so few nights. Her heart seemed to ache from all of the time spent alone in this old house. At twenty two, this was not how she had pictured her life.

For years, she'd been a teacher in a little white schoolhouse on Martha's Vineyard. It was her passion and she loved the children. Still single at twenty-seven, she had convinced herself that teaching was her calling. With a bit of regret, she had accepted the fact she might never marry and convinced herself she was okay with that.

While all of her childhood girlfriends had beautiful weddings and started families of their own, she found herself alone every night, eating supper by herself, correcting spelling papers. Until that day in the market, that wonderful day she had met her Albert.

She knew she had found her soul mate the moment she peered into those magnificent brown eyes. This delightfully handsome stranger had made her feel alive and she knew she would give up everything she had known to share a life with him.

As he hobbled along the dock, securing the boat, he could hear the boys' laughter and was thankful to have two devoted sons who loved the fisherman's life as much as he did. They worked hard and were skilled at finding and catching the hard shells. After so many years on the sea, they were good enough to do the job on their own now.

They had been chasing the lobster with him for almost twenty years and were more than ready to run their own vessel. He knew they wanted to modernize his boat. Ennis had come to him with catalogues filled with meters and gauges and newfangled contraptions that promised to make their lives easier and the business more profitable.

Albert would shake his head and toss the magazines in the trash. He did not like change. Stoically, he did things as his father had taught him. It had worked for his father and it was working for them. Albert knew it was not only change he feared, but the thought of not being needed on his own boat anymore scared him. He was afraid the gadgets would replace his good sense and intuition. Ennis and Shane could fill the boat just as quickly without his constant nagging and complaining, and then where would that leave him?

They were below deck now, preparing to unload and get the lobster to market, a job he was thankful to surrender a few years back. It would be another eight hours before they would feel the warm comfort of their beds.

By this time, Albert would be waking up to the smell of hotcakes and fresh brewed coffee being served up by his smiling wife. He vowed to himself to spend the entire day with her. They would walk hand and hand into town and he'd buy her a bunch of daisies, her favorite. They would go to lunch and enjoy catching up on the things he'd missed while out on this trip.

Albert knew in his heart, though, that in reality he would probably spend the next couple days nursing his weathered body back to health, and she would be there beside him, rubbing his back and bringing him hot tea with honey. Yes, she was a good woman. He would make it a point to tell her so…. tomorrow.

He could hear Shane talking above the sound of the surf, "Ennis, ya know it's time fa us to staat our own business. Papa will neva give us dis boat"

Albert felt a little weak in the knees as Shane returned an answer. "Yep, we have enough money socked away now. I think we should tell him before the next trip."

Albert's head was spinning, his breathing heavy. He felt as though he might fall into the ocean. *How can they leave me?* He thought to himself. *What will I do? I can't do it alone.* His mind was racing. He had always planned to give the boat to his sons. He just hadn't planned to do it so soon.

Standing up, he walked toward the shore with his head hanging and his heart breaking. As the daylight faded into twilight, Albert made his way home. As he approached the house, he could see the smoke puffing out of the chimney and the lights burning in the windows. As always, he could not wait to walk in the door and see her smiling face.

He would hug her and tell her all of the things he had held inside. It was time to give his boat to the boys and find a job in town. They would spend so much time together. This would make Catherine happy and Shane and Ennis as well.

He could not wait to walk in the door and share the news.

Back at the house, Catherine had folded the last of the laundry she had taken off of the line. The kitchen smelled of roasted chicken and potatoes. There was a pot of fresh, coffee brewing on the stove. Albert loved his coffee and she always made it a point to have a cup ready and waiting for him when he walked through the door. Today, however, he would have to pour it himself. Wistfully, she stood there in her kitchen, where she had stood a thousand times before, and looked around.

Thoughtfully, she placed a plate in front of Albert's chair and laid the silverware alongside it on a fresh linen napkin, one that was reserved for holidays and special company. The tears began to force their way out of the corners of her faded blue eyes as she pulled the note she had so carefully written out of her apron pocket and laid it on top of the dinner plate, folded in half.

My dearest Albert,

I have spent the best years of my life taking care of you and our boys. I gave up who I was and all I had. I don't feel needed anymore and I don't feel loved. I don't even feel at home in this house...in your life. I feel lost and alone. I will always love you, but I must find myself. I must find my place. Goodbye, Albert. I wish you only the best.

With that, Catherine slipped on her warmest fall jacket and wrapped a scarf around her neck. Sighing, she picked up the weathered brown suitcase and made her way to the front door. The neighbor gently took her suitcase from her hand and slid it into the back seat of the idling sedan. Over the past year, she had stashed away enough money for a train ticket. Before settling into the back seat next to her suitcase, she turned for one last look at what had been her life.

"I will miss you," she whispered to herself, "but it was time."

The Fountain

"I was suddenly quite overwhelmed with the multitude of coins below and the hope this hidden fountain of dreams had brought to so many deprived or needy souls."

I could hear, in the distance, the whisper of running water as I made my way down the little dirt path. I'd decided to spend the day exploring a new park in my community. I enjoyed the peace and tranquility of this little adventure, surprised at just how remarkably quiet it really was. It was so serene, I felt as if I might be the last person on earth as I proceeded down the footpath.

The sound intensified as I reached the bottom of the hill and followed the trail around a sharp corner. Suddenly, an unexpected mist covered my face as I came upon a magnificent stone fountain sitting stoically, yet looking very out of place, in the middle of a large, circular pond. Finding myself quite taken aback by the spectacle before me, I stood mesmerized for a moment or two before venturing onward for a closer look.

The fountain, which was at least twenty feet tall, towered before me with a fresh, clear waterfall spilling out and over the top into the welcoming pool below. As I stepped up to the little cement wall encircling the entire body of water, I leaned inquisitively over the edge and could not help but notice the sparkling reflection of something shining beneath the surface.

Upon closer scrutiny, I found myself staring at a sea of glittering coins as vast and abundant as any pirate's treasure. The assortment of dimes, quarters, nickels, and pennies ensconced the bottom of the pond, and I realized I had inadvertently discovered a wishing fountain.

At that moment, it occurred to me that this was quite a fitting discovery, since the past couple years of my life had indeed centered on hope, prayers, and wishes. As I reached into my pocket in search of a coin, I recalled the many lonely days spent seeking the strength to lose the massive amount of weight that suffocated my soul and had stolen so many irreplaceable experiences from my life. I remember longing for the self-will to escape the firm grip that both alcohol and food had somehow seized over my morose mind and hopeless spirit.

I'd spent countless hours regretting my thoughtless decision to abandon my college education and forsake a lifelong dream of writing books and stories for others to enjoy. Oh, how I longed for the chance to complete my education.

There had been many smaller, yet very significant wishes, too. They were, for the most part, simple dreams to do things most people take for granted such as a leisurely trip to the zoo or a weekend camping trip under the stars, enjoying a toasted marshmallow or a hot dog roasted on a stick, while telling stories around a raging campfire.

I can remember wondering how it might feel to ride a Ferris wheel to the top of the earth and see the rest of the world scurry about below as the wind blew through my hair and the sun kissed my face. Just then, I came upon the only coin on my person—a single copper penny.

Holding the shiny penny in my hand, I stared out into the sea of hopes and dreams and wondered how many people had stood right here, in silent desperation, contemplating their own aspirations and desires while taking great pains to select the appropriate wish. I was suddenly quite overwhelmed with the multitude of coins below and the hope this hidden fountain of dreams had brought to so many deprived or needy souls.

And then it happened. I began to count my blessings. The past few years had been kind to me. I had lost nearly one hundred fifty pounds along with my dependency on alcohol. With these significant changes, I had been afforded the opportunity to regain my freedom, thus finding myself back in college after two decades of regret. I was writing again and had spent my entire summer going places and doing things I had never done before, including a trip to the zoo and an enjoyable weekend camping adventure. Yes, I had celebrated a remarkable year.

I stared at the penny, not really knowing what to wish for. After all, I had been quite fortunate to have witnessed so many of my own dreams come true; so lucky in fact, that it seemed wrong to steal a wish from someone else.

I had discovered within myself the strength to create my own destiny, the power to make my own dreams come true, and the patience to wait for miracles to happen. I remained for just a moment longer, and then I slipped the penny back into my pocket, thinking to myself, *perhaps I will leave the magic here for someone else*, and with that I headed back up the path toward home.

The Attic

"All of the cherished relics from my past seem to lie there staring at me, still waiting for their chance to shine"

I open the attic door and begin my ascent up the ancient staircase. The boards creak and moan beneath me as I make my way to the top. As I rise, so does the temperature, and I feel the perspiration seep out of the pores on the back of my neck. Rolling down my shirt sleeve, I wipe my arm across my damp forehead, breathing a sigh of relief when I finally reach the top stair. Panting, I appreciate why I had not attempted this expedition before I'd lost two hundred fifty pounds, convinced it would have resulted in a stop, drop, and roll which had nothing to do with fire!

As I stand at the top, looking around and struggling to catch my breath, I slowly turn my head from side to side, observing the room around me. It is as though I have stepped out of a time machine and back to the life I'd had before my battle with food and alcohol. My eyes begin to adjust to the muted tones of grays and black and I notice the single light bulb hanging from a wire in the center of the very warm and stifling space.

I reach for the chain, pull it, and as the light snaps on, the room seems to come to life. My eyes land upon the exquisite Gibson guitar which rests in the corner. I can see myself sitting on my bed as a teenager, plucking away at the strings, trying to play along to the records blaring from the tiny speakers of my RCA phonograph.

To my right, I see the drafting table which I had so diligently saved my pennies to purchase. Upon it sits a sizeable box filled with colored pencils, charcoal, brushes, and poster paint, along with a stack of sketch books and drafting paper. I was, at one time, planning to be a cartoonist and work for Walt Disney, inventing wonderful characters who would one day come to life upon the big screen.

Beneath the table lay tennis racquets and golf clubs, and I gasp just a little when I spot my red and faded leather baseball glove lying there on the floor. This is the same glove that had led my high school softball team to four straight regional championships with me on the mound. My red and white varsity jacket hangs upon the wall above it, covered in a clear, thin sheath of plastic, the hard earned awards and medals still shiny underneath. I glance around and see the empty notebooks and journals whose pages have turned yellow while waiting for my imagination to bring them to life.

Feeling empty and melancholy, I stand there, in a room full of broken dreams, distraught over the demise of all these hopes and aspirations. Quietly, I grieve for all I had given up and thrown away because I had permitted food to take over and rule my life. The room begins to feel like a purgatory of sorts…a place where time stands still and nothing ever changes. All of the cherished relics from my past seem to lie there staring at me, still waiting for their chance to shine.

Hanging my head in utter sadness, I reach up and pull the chain, leaving them all in gloomy darkness once again. A tear falls from the corner of my eye as I head for the staircase. Stopping for just a moment, I pause to look at the old six string sitting in the corner, then walk over and lift it protectively into my arms. As I slip the worn out plastic pick from between the strings, my fingers slide quite naturally into a C-chord position and I gently strum the magnificent instrument. The tone is rich and clear and I can't help but grin as I bend to set it back in the corner. Holding on to it, though, unable to let go, I think to myself, *perhaps this ol g itar li e m self still has a song or two left in it.* Maybe all it needs is someone who cares enough to listen.

With that, I smile and nod to myself as I slip my arm through the strap and sling it over my shoulder and onto my back, feeling much like an 80's rock star. I stick the pick in my pocket and head, whistling, down the stairs.

Cupcakes & Snowflakes

"Along with the Indian summer, there had been many other unexpected experiences this year. Finding one another had been the phenomenon which had set into motion a series of events that would change both of our lives forever."

We sat upon a broken oak which had fallen last year during a raging thunderstorm. Relaxed and quite content, we rested near the drifting river, relishing in the extreme comfort we had found in the company of one another. Blissfully, we reflected in subtle silence while watching the last of the red and yellow leaves of autumn fall and spin wildly to the ground from above. As I held her tender hand in humble adoration, she shifted and huddled closer to me in an effort to ward off the early evening chill.

I wrapped my arm around her shoulder and pulled her close as we sat in awe and enjoyed the most breathtaking sunset of this unexpected Indian summer. The blazing orange and ginger sky had brought to mind our conversation from the night before when we had roasted marshmallows together on broken sticks in front of a raging campfire.

Along with the Indian summer, there had been many other unexpected experiences this year. Finding one another had been the phenomenon which had set into motion a series of events that would change both of our lives forever.

On the surface, one would say we were mismatched, incompatible, and even lopsided. Looking back, we might respectfully agree and then, of course, laugh at the asymmetric appearance of our unusual little romance...for laughing, you see, was the reliable, dependable, foolproof secret to our happiness. The magic could be found in the sheer absurdity of our unforeseen connection. The truth is, the random unpredictability of our romance is exactly what fueled its fire. Ahhh yes, back to the fire.

We had stared into the sky that evening, feeling the exhilaration and pure joy that a new romance brings, when we saw it fall—a star which dropped swiftly from the sky to the darkness beyond the horizon. "Make a wish," she had whispered into my ear.

I closed my eyes and dreamed of castles and magic and riches beyond one's wildest imagination. When I opened them, I found her staring back at me, smiling that magnificent smile that never failed to take my breath away. The glorious innocence I found there made my head swoon. She looked at me and softly said…"What did you wish for, my love?" Unable to speak I sighed, "You first."

She held my hands in hers and said, "I wished for you and me to spend eternity together sharing sunsets and seasons and cupcakes…lots and lots of cupcakes. I hoped for kisses in the rain and dancing in the morning sun. Most importantly, I prayed for the strength to face the harshest of winters together, doing battle with the wicked snowstorms, while catching snowflakes on our tongues and laughing….always, always laughing."

Astonished and enchanted, I found myself speechless yet smitten with this woman who saw the world through such simple naivety and innocence. I felt humbled and humiliated with myself for my own selfish wishes and desires. A tear slipped from my eye as I stared at her breathtaking beauty and I suddenly realized that a lifetime of snowflakes and cupcakes sounded quite perfect to me.

About the Author

In 1994 I made a huge career change. I quit my job and decided to open a bar. Not just any bar, but a gay/lesbian show bar. I immersed my entire being in the nightclub scene, and yes indeed, it was a "gay" old time I had. I found myself living a life of excess.

I drank too much, ate too much, partied too much, dated too many, and spent much more money than I had. After 17 years of abuse, my body almost self-destructed. At one point, I found myself weighing in at 528 pounds, an alcoholic, broke, and alone. I sat there on my little corner of "rock bottom" and felt sorry for myself. I was repulsed and ashamed of what I had become. On January 15, 2012, I had an epiphany. I was forced to face the reality of my mortality and I was mortified.

On January 16, 2012, I quit drinking completely, which was truly difficult in that I still owned a bar. I lost a total of 252 pounds and went back to college after 25 years. I am also a loud and proud lesbian. I have stared almost every type of discrimination in the eye and vanquished it. I have lived life to the highest of highs and hit the lowest of lows. I am still searching for my middle ground. I have completely turned my life around.

I am not who I was three years ago. I like to write and create. My passion is to communicate, educate, and motivate. Recently, I lost my best friend and my greatest supporter, my mother. She was never one to whine or engage in self-pity. Despite all of the hardships she herself endured, she managed to raise 4 very strong, independent and successful children. When we were overwhelmed with stress, love, and life she would sit us down and calmly say "Pick a struggle, cupcake...and resolve it".

I did...I have....and now I would love to share some of my experiences, struggles, failures, and triumphs with you. In doing this, I hope to compel and inspire you to confront your demons and conquer your looming catastrophes. There is always an answer, an escape, or a solution. We just have to find it! Together, we shall! Now, let's get started! Pick a struggle, cupcake.....pick a struggle.

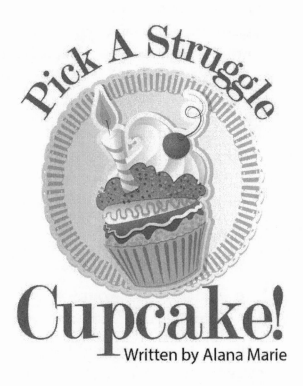

Pick A Struggle Cupcake!

Written by Alana Marie

ISBN-10: 1503000680
Pick a Struggle Cupcake Blog

Where it all started.
www.PickaStruggleCupcake.com

38640487R00111

Made in the USA
Charleston, SC
15 February 2015